# First World War
## and Army of Occupation
# War Diary
## France, Belgium and Germany

36 DIVISION
109 Infantry Brigade
Royal Inniskilling Fusiliers
2nd Battalion
1 February 1918 - 30 April 1919

WO95/2510/2

The Naval & Military Press Ltd
www.nmarchive.com
**Published in association with The National Archives**

Published by

## The Naval & Military Press Ltd

Unit 10 Ridgewood Industrial Park,

Uckfield, East Sussex,

TN22 5QE England

Tel: +44 (0) 1825 749494

www.naval-military-press.com

www.nmarchive.com

*This diary has been reprinted in facsimile from the original. Any imperfections are inevitably reproduced and the quality may fall short of modern type and cartographic standards.*

**© Crown Copyright**
**Images reproduced by permission of The National Archives, London, England, 2015.**

# Contents

| Document type | Place/Title | Date From | Date To |
|---|---|---|---|
| Heading | WO95/2510/2 | | |
| Heading | 36th Division 109th Infy Bde 2nd Bn Roy. Innis. Fus. Feb 1918-Apr 1919 From 32 Div 96 Bde | | |
| Heading | 2nd Royal Inniskilling Fusiliers War Diary For Month Of February, 1918 Vol 43 | | |
| War Diary | Ham | 01/02/1918 | 01/02/1918 |
| War Diary | Villeselve | 02/02/1918 | 02/02/1918 |
| War Diary | Fluquieres | 03/02/1918 | 22/02/1918 |
| War Diary | Artemps | 23/02/1918 | 28/02/1918 |
| War Diary | | 27/02/1918 | 27/02/1918 |
| Heading | 109th Brigade 36th Division 2nd Battalion Royal Inniskilling Fusiliers March 1918 | | |
| Heading | 2nd Royal Inniskilling Fusiliers War Diary For Month Of March 1918 Vol 44 | | |
| War Diary | | 01/03/1918 | 30/03/1918 |
| Heading | 109th Brigade 36th Division 2nd Battalion Royal Inniskilling Fusiliers April 1918. | | |
| Heading | 2nd Royal Inniskilling Fusiliers War Diary For Month Of April 1918 Vol 45 | | |
| War Diary | | 01/04/1918 | 30/04/1918 |
| Heading | 2nd Royal Inniskilling Fusiliers War Diary For Month Of May, 1918 Vol 46 | | |
| War Diary | Brielen | 01/05/1918 | 06/05/1918 |
| War Diary | Canal Bk | 06/05/1918 | 15/05/1918 |
| War Diary | Brielen | 15/05/1918 | 21/05/1918 |
| War Diary | Canal Bk | 22/05/1918 | 27/05/1918 |
| War Diary | Brielen | 27/05/1918 | 31/05/1918 |
| Miscellaneous | War Diary Of 2nd Bn. Royal Inniskilling Fuslrs. From 1st June 1918 To 30th June 1918 (Volume 47) | | |
| War Diary | Sheet 28 N.W. | 01/06/1918 | 01/06/1918 |
| War Diary | Sheet 27 | 03/06/1918 | 06/06/1918 |
| War Diary | Tunnelling Camp | 07/06/1918 | 21/06/1918 |
| War Diary | Peterboro Camp | 21/06/1918 | 30/06/1918 |
| Heading | War Diary Of 2nd Battalion Royal Inniskilling Fusiliers From 1st July 1918 To 31st July 1918 (Volume 48) | | |
| War Diary | | 01/07/1918 | 31/07/1918 |
| Heading | War Diary Of Volume 48 August 1918 2nd Bn. Royal Inniskilling Fusiliers Vol 49 | | |
| War Diary | | 01/08/1918 | 31/08/1918 |
| Heading | War Diary Of 2nd Royal Inniskilling Fusiliers From 1st Sept 1918 To 30th Sept 1918 Vol 50 | | |
| Heading | War Diary Of 2nd Battalion Royal Inniskilling Fuslrs From 1st September To 30th September 1918 Volume 50 | | |
| War Diary | | 01/09/1918 | 02/09/1918 |
| War Diary | Mikokereele | 02/09/1918 | 26/09/1918 |
| Heading | War Diary Of The 2nd Battalion Royal Inniskilling Fusiliers From October 1st To October 31st 1918 Volume 51 | | |
| War Diary | Reference Map Sheet 28 N.E.4. Dadizeele 1/10000 | 01/10/1918 | 05/10/1918 |

| | | | |
|---|---|---|---|
| War Diary | Reference Map Sheet 28 N.W. 1/20.000 | 06/10/1918 | 11/10/1918 |
| War Diary | Reference Map Sheet 28 N.E.4 | 12/10/1918 | 14/10/1918 |
| War Diary | Reference Map Sheet 29 | 14/10/1918 | 31/10/1918 |
| Miscellaneous | Appendix No. 1 | | |
| Miscellaneous | Appendix No. 2 | 02/10/1918 | 02/10/1918 |
| Miscellaneous | Appendix No. 3 | | |
| Heading | War Diary Of 2nd Bn. Royal Inniskilling Fusiliers For The Month Of November, 1918 | | |
| War Diary | St Anne | 01/11/1918 | 30/11/1918 |
| Heading | War Diary Of The 2nd Bn. Royal Inniskilling Fusiliers For The Month Of December 1918 | | |
| War Diary | | 01/12/1918 | 31/01/1919 |
| War Diary | Roncq | 01/02/1919 | 01/03/1919 |
| War Diary | Mouscron | 02/03/1919 | 30/04/1919 |

worm 25/25/10 (2)

worm 25/25/10 (2)

**36TH DIVISION**
**109TH INFY BDE**

2ND BN ROY. INNIS. FUS.

FEB 1918-APR 1919

From 32 Div
96 Bde

2nd Royal Inniskilling Fusiliers.

WAR DIARY

for

MONTH OF FEBRUARY, 1918.

# WAR DIARY
## INTELLIGENCE SUMMARY

Army Form C. 2118.

| Place | Date 1918 | Hour | Summary of Events and Information | Remarks and references to Appendices |
|---|---|---|---|---|
| HAM. | Feb. 1 | | Battalion arrived in HAM at 10 am. where it was met by Major Broadbent, 36th Division. Guides had been provided and the Battalion marched to VILLESELVE where they arrived about 2 pm - the Transport arriving about two hours later. On the march from HAM the battalion was met by Brig-General HESSEY, D.S.O. and at VILLESELVE by the Staff Captain 109th Brigade and Captain Hodgson, a/G.S.O.1 36th Division. Billets were arranged for by the 11th Royal Innis.Fus. and the battalion was soon comfortably settled down. | Rev. Major First Ord & Brookes. S.A.2 S.A.2 S.A.2 S.A. |
| VILLESELVE | Feb. 2 | | Was devoted to cleaning up and preparing for the march to the 109th Brigade. | |
| FLUQUIERES | Feb. 3 | | Battalion paraded at 8.30 am and marched to FLUQUIRES - about a half a mile from the village the band of the 10th Royal.Innis.Fus. was waiting and played the battalion into billets. On arrival in the village the battalion was met by Lieut-Col. Lord A.K.Farnham, Comdg., 10th Royal Innis.Fus. and officers of the 10th Battalion., also Lieut-Col. Rigg, D.S.O. who had come on ahead. The battalion marched straight to their billets and shortly afterwards the 10th Battn. less 150 men who had been posted to us marched out. In the afternoon several of the officers and men of the 2nd Battn went to AUBIGNY to watch the final of the Brigade Football Competition which was won by "D" Coy 10th Battn who beat the 173rd Bde R.F.A. 4 - 2. | S.A.E. |
| | Feb. 3 - 15 | | Battalion remained in FLUQUIERES and were engaged on working parties on the Battle Zone. Officers and N.C.Os reconnoitred the line daily. | |

Army Form C. 2118.

# WAR DIARY
## or
## INTELLIGENCE SUMMARY.
*(Erase heading not required.)*

Instructions regarding War Diaries and Intelligence Summaries are contained in F. S. Regs., Part II. and the Staff Manual respectively. Title pages will be prepared in manuscript.

| Place | Date 1918 | Hour | Summary of Events and Information | Remarks and references to Appendices |
|---|---|---|---|---|
| FLUQUIERES | Feb.5 | | Lieut-Col.Bigg,D.S.O. was called to the War Office by wire. As many of the battalion as possible paraded to bid him goodbye. He gave those present a short address and after saying goodbye rode away. | AL. |
| | Feb.10 | | Major-General Nugent,C.B.,D.S.O.,Commdg.36th Division, inspected the battalion in full marching order, also Regimental Transport. After a very minute inspection he complimented the battalion on its turnout, a special word of praise being given to the Transport. | AL. |
| | Feb.13 | | Lieut-Col.Lord A.K.Fernham took over Command of the battalion. | AL. |
| | Feb.15 | | Divisional Commander lectured all officers and the senior N.C.Os.of the Brigade at GRAND SERAUCOURT on the principles of the Defence of the Line and the enemy intentions. Battalion marched from FLUQUIERES and relieved the 15th Bn. R.Irish Rifles in Brigade Reserve.   ← SERAUCOURT. | AL. |
| | Feb.16-22 | | Battalion remained in Brigade Reserve and was employed on work in the Battle Zone. | AL. |
| | Feb.22 | | The Battalion withdrew from Brigade Reserve and moved to ARTEMPS where they remained for the night. | AL. |
| ARTEMPS | Feb.23 | | Was devoted to cleaning up and preparing for the line. An Officers V Sergeants Football Match was hurriedly arranged and proved very interesting and amusing. Sergts.winning by 4 goals to 2. Teams - Officers, Col Lieut-Col.Lord A.K.Fernham, Backs Capt.Morony and Lieut.Cox. Half-Backs Lieuts.Power,Clarke,O'Ryan, Forwards - 2/Lts.Watson,Capt.Burke,2/Lts.Sharpley,Brown,McConnell. | AL. GROUPIES A.3 &c, B. |

**Army Form C. 2118.**

# WAR DIARY
## *or*
## INTELLIGENCE SUMMARY.
*(Erase heading not required.)*

| Place | Date 1918 | Hour | Summary of Events and Information | Remarks and references to Appendices |
|---|---|---|---|---|
| | Feb. 23 | | Sergeants - Goel C.Q.M.S., Godfrey. Backs - Sgt.Hell & Sgt.Ellism Half-Backs - Sergts. Reid, Neil, Henderson. Forwards - Sergts. Gracey, Turkington, Creswell, Burke and C.Q.M.S. Hell. | S.A.2. |
| | | | The battalion paraded at 5 pm and marched to the line where they relieved the 9th Royal Innis.Fus. The 15th Bn.Royal Irish Rifles on the right (107th Bde.) and the 15th King's Liverpool Regt., 30th Division, on the left. | S.A.2. |
| | Feb. 23-28. | | In the line. - "A" Coy Right Front holding, from B 8 c 86 - B 7 a 96. 35 with company Hqrs at B 7 c 8.5. | S.A.2. |
| | | | "B" Coy Left Front holding from B 7 a 96.25 - The ST. QUENTIN CANAL company Hqrs at A 12 a 9.7. | S.A.2. |
| | | | "C" Coy Counter attack Company, GRUGIES, and holding the Keeps. Company Hqrs at A 18 c 4.7. | S.A.2. |
| | | | "D" Coy, Passive Defence, at A.17.d.7.4. close to Battn.H'qtrs. | S.A.2. |
| | Feb. 27 | | Inter-Company relief "C" Coy relieving "A" Coy, and "D" Coy relieving "B" Coy. | S.A.2. |
| | | | Casualties during tour - 2 Other Ranks wounded. | |

S.J. Logan Major
for O.C.Gd
2nd Royal Inniskillings 2/3/18
2 Royal Fusiliers

109th Brigade.
36th Division.
----------

2nd BATTALION

ROYAL INNISKILLING FUSILIERS

M A R C H   1 9 1 8

109/36

Vol. 44

2ND ROYAL INNISKILLING FUSILIERS.

WAR DIARY

FOR

MONTH OF MARCH 1918.

Army Form C. 2118.

# WAR DIARY

## ~~INTELLIGENCE SUMMARY~~

2nd Royal Inniskilling Fusilrs

*(Erase heading not required.)*

Instructions regarding War Diaries and Intelligence Summaries are contained in F. S. Regs., Part II. and the Staff Manual respectively. Title pages will be prepared in manuscript.

| Place | Date 1918 | Hour | Summary of Events and Information | Remarks and references to Appendices |
|---|---|---|---|---|
| | Mar. 1 | | The Battalion still in the Line. - "C" Coy Right Front. "D" " Left " "A" Coy, Counter Attack Company and holding the Keeps. "B" Coy, Passive Defence at A.17.d.7.4. close to Battalion Headquarters. | |
| | " 2 | | In the line. Casualties during tour 1 Officer, 2nd Lieut. Brown, KILLED, 2 Other Ranks wounded. | |
| | " 3 - 4 | | The Battalion was relieved by the 1st Bn.Royal Inniskilling Fus. and marched to ARTEMPS where they were billeted. | |
| | " 4 | | In billets at ARTEMPS. Day devoted to cleaning up etc. | |
| | " 5 | | In billets at ARTEMPS. One Company employed on working parties. Remainder of Companies training under Coy arrangements. Specialist training was also carried out under the various instructors. | |
| | " 6 | | In billets at ARTEMPS. - ditto - | |
| | " 7 | | - ditto - - ditto - | |
| | " 8 - 10 | | - ditto - - ditto - | |
| | " 11 | | - ditto - - ditto - | |

Army Form C. 2118.

# WAR DIARY
## or
## INTELLIGENCE SUMMARY.
(Erase heading not required.)

| Place | Date | Hour | Summary of Events and Information | Remarks and references to Appendices |
|---|---|---|---|---|
| | 1918 Mar.11/12 | | The Battalion was relieved by the 1st Bn.R.Innis.Fus. and moved to HAMEL and took over billets vacated by 9th Bn.R.Innis.Fus. | |
| | " 12 | | In billets at HAMEL. Companies employed on Working Parties. The training of Specialists was carried out under the various instructors. | |
| | " 13/16 | | In billets at HAMEL. - ditto. | |
| | " 16 | | A Boxing Tournament was held on the evening of the 16th inst. when some very good amateur talent displayed - four weights being represented - Heavy, Welter, Middle and Light Weights.<br>Lieut-Colonel Lord Farnham - Referee.<br>Lieut.Cox,M.C. and Pte.Quinn - Judges.<br>Capt.G.M.Burke - Timekeeper.<br><br>Prizes were distributed at the Sports on the 17th March 1918 (St.Patrick's Day). | |
| | " 17 | | St.Patrick's Day. In the morning Shamrock was issued to all ranks in the Battalion. The day was observed as a holiday and a holiday and Combined Sports (1st and 2nd Battns.) were held. The officers were at Home to their friends, as were also the Sergeants. The principal events of the day were :-<br>Tug-of-War, Catch Weights - Inter Battalion. Won by 2nd Battn.<br>Cross Country Run - " - Won by 2nd Battn.<br>Football Match - " - Won by 2nd Battn.<br>One Mile Race - " - Won by 2nd Battn.<br>Hidden Treasure Race - " - do -<br>A most successful and enjoyable day was concluded at about 6.30 pm when prizes were distributed by Brig-Gen.W.F.Hessey,D.S.O. | |

Army Form C. 2118.

# WAR DIARY
## or
## INTELLIGENCE SUMMARY.
(Erase heading not required.)

Instructions regarding War Diaries and Intelligence Summaries are contained in F. S. Regs., Part II. and the Staff Manual respectively. Title pages will be prepared in manuscript.

| Place | Date 1918 | Hour | Summary of Events and Information | Remarks and references to Appendices |
|---|---|---|---|---|
| | Mar.18 | | In billets at HAMEL. Companies employed on working parties, and training of specialists. | |
| | " " | 19/20 | The Battalion paraded at 5 pm and marched to the Line where they relieved the 9th Bn.R.Innis.Fus | |
| | " 21 | | On the morning of the 21st inst. a terrific bombardment was opened by the enemy about 4.30 am - this continued throughout the day - At 10 am Transport and Quartermaster's Stores were ordered to leave ARIEMPS and proceed to TUGNY, where they bivouacked outside the village. At 9 pm. orders were received to proceed to BROUCHY arrived there at 2 am 22/3/18. Details of Battalion left out of the line (Classes of Instruction Specialists, Drums etc.) left ARIEMPS at 10.30 am and proceed to BRAY CHRISTOPHE under command of 2nd Lieut.J.B.McConnell and 2nd Lieut. J.M.J.Martin. At this place the details were organized into Coys and Platoons etc. and came under command of Lieut-Col.Cox, Rifle Bde. About 8 pm.same day Details proceeded to AUBIGNY where a Composite Battalion was formed of all details "36th Division under command of Major Montgomery, D.S.O.,15th Royal Irish Rifles. - No.1 Company consisted of details of 2nd Bn.Royal Inniskilling Fusiliers under 2nd Lieut.J.B.McConnell. | |
| | " 22 | | This Battn left Aubigny about 12 noon 22nd and proceeded to DURY, where it established outpost petrols, Bridge guards during the remainder of the day. About midnight all outposts were withdrawn across the Canal and took up position in Strong Points etc. already prepared. Transport and Q.M's Stores left BROUCHY about 9 am and marched to GUISCARD and bivouacked. | |

Army Form C. 2118.

# WAR DIARY
## or
## INTELLIGENCE SUMMARY.
(Erase heading not required.)

Instructions regarding War Diaries and Intelligence Summaries are contained in F. S. Regs., Part II. and the Staff Manual respectively. Title pages will be prepared in manuscript.

| Place | Date | Hour | Summary of Events and Information | Remarks and references to Appendices |
|---|---|---|---|---|
| | Mar.23 1918 | | Transport and Q.M's Stores left GUISCARD about 9 am, all personnel of the Transport and Q.M's Stores being formed up into two platoons and moved back into Reserve to two platoons similiarly formed from Transport personnel of 1st Battn.R.Innis.Fus. At 9.30 pm orders were received to move forward and attack AUBIGNY. A heavy mist prevailed on the morning of the 23rd when the Composite battalion was heavily attacked about 11 am.- the position was held until about 2 pm, when owing to the left flank being pushed back we were compelled to withdraw to BROUCHY, where we took up position on the outskirts of the village which were held during the day. Enemy Aircraft was very active over this position - flying very low and using machine gun fire both on the position and thro' the streets of the village. On leaving DURY No.1 Coy (2nd R. Innis Fus Details) were detailed to cover the retirement of the remainder of the Battalion, but since that nothing has been heard of them | |
| | "24 | | At 8 am Transport and Q.M's Stores personnel marched off and when entering GOOLANCOURT the enemy opened machine gun fire causing several casualties. The troops fell back in good order and took up position at Cross roads near GUISCARD, they then moved forward and took up positions in trenches supporting some French troops. About 5 pm the enemy attacked causing both flanks to retire, but the right flank shortly afterwards re-established the line. At 10 pm the troops were withdrawn to a position in the rear. On the 24th the position of the Composite Battalion was maintained until about 3 pm when it was compelled to retire thro' VILLESELVES where it joined the French Troops. The retirement was caused by the units on the left flank giving ground - the position at this time was very critical as the battalion was | |

# WAR DIARY or INTELLIGENCE SUMMARY

Army Form C. 2118.

| Place | Date 1918 | Hour | Summary of Events and Information | Remarks and references to Appendices |
|---|---|---|---|---|
| | Mar 24 | | partially surrounded. - A Cavalry Charge temporarily restored the position and enabled the retirement to be carried out successfully.<br>After retiring through the French lines the battalion was disbanded and men ordered to join their own units at Transport Lines. | |
| | 25 | | At 2 am on the morning 25th Transport and Q.M's Stores personnel relieved by French Troops marched to rejoin Transport at AVRICOURT. All d tails 2nd R.Innis.Fus at this time came under command of Captain A.L.Haire.<br>At 3 pm marched to GUERBIGNY arriving there about 2 am 26th inst. On the 25th the battalion marched to WARSY under command of Captain A.L.Haire and were billeted. | |
| | 26 | | On the morning of the/battalion marched from WARSY and took up position about 2 kilos N.E. of GUERBIGNY. - this position was held until the morning of the 27th. | |
| | 27 | | About 8 am the enemy attacked compelling both flanks to retire across the River AVRE. The battalion fought a rear guard action to enable remainder of Brigade to withdraw across the river.- Eventually the bn.retired through the French and billeted in BOULLANCOURT, where stragglers rejoined. | |
| | 28 | | Marched to GRIVESNES arriving there about 11 am. At 2 pm ordered to take up outpost line East of COULLEMELLE. | |
| | 29 | | Relieved by French Troops and marched to EPAGNY. At 8 pm marched to WAILLY arriving there about 4 am. 30th. | |
| | 30 | | Marched to CALEUX and entrained for EU at 9 am 31/3/18, arriving 5 pm and marched to MENESLIES and were billeted. | |

Army Form C. 2118.

# WAR DIARY
or
# INTELLIGENCE SUMMARY.
(Erase heading not required.)

| Place | Date | Hour | Summary of Events and Information | Remarks and references to Appendices |
|---|---|---|---|---|
| | Mar. | 1918 | The marching of the men and their behaviour under fire was excellent throughout the whole operations.<br><br>Total casualties during the whole operations were :-<br><br>    Officers - Wounded 3<br>                 Missing 21.<br><br>    Other Ranks - Killed 7<br>                   Wounded 15.<br>                   Missing 646. | |

Cmdg. 2nd Royal Inniskilling Fus.

109th Brigade.
36th Division.
------------

2nd BATTALION

ROYAL INNISKILLING FUSILIERS

APRIL 1918.

Account of withdrawal with Brigade H.Q. Diary.

# 2ND ROYAL INNISKILLING FUSILIERS.

## WAR DIARY for MONTH OF APRIL, 1918.

Army Form C. 2118.

# WAR DIARY
## INTELLIGENCE SUMMARY. 2nd Bn. Royal Inniskilling Fusrs.
*(Erase heading not required.)*

| Place | Date 1918 | Hour | Summary of Events and Information | Remarks and references to Appendices |
|---|---|---|---|---|
| | 1st April | | Battalion in billets at MENESLIES. | |
| | 2/3rd | | Battalion in billets at MENESLIES. Capt J Colhoun MC rejoined the Batn from hospital and took over Command of the Battalion from Capt D Stone who took over the duties of Second-in-Command | |
| | 4th | | Battalion in billets at MENESLIES. A draft of 12 Officers:- Major E.H. Barton  2/Lt. J.A. Cockey<br>Capt. S.M.A. Mark     " P.W. de C. Smale<br>Lieut H.H. Sinokay<br>2/Lt. M.C. Beale       " W. Tylor<br>" E Sharkey            " E.M. Phillips<br>" W.P. Johnston      " C. Taylor<br>                              " W.B. Dukes<br>and 107 Other Ranks joined the Battalion from the 2nd Inniskilling Battn | |
| | 4/5th | | Entrained about 11pm at NOICOURT. Detrained at ROUSBRUGGE at 4pm 5th inst. Battalion moved by motor Lorries | |

Army Form C. 2118.

# WAR DIARY
## or
## INTELLIGENCE SUMMARY.
*(Erase heading not required.)*

| Place | Date 1918 | Hour | Summary of Events and Information | Remarks and references to Appendices |
|---|---|---|---|---|
| | | | | BELGIUM Sheet 28 N.W. |
| | 4/5" April | | to DIRTY BUCKET CAMP and billeted there. | B.19 c 2.3.7. |
| | 6th " | | In billets at DIRTY BUCKET Camp. Battalion moved to CANAL BANK (SUPPORT BRIGADE AREA) about 3 p.m. on the evening of the 6th inst. | |
| | 7th " | | In billets at CANAL BANK. Training under Company arrangements was carried out. Draft of 308 Other Ranks joined the Batt. | C.25 a 2.3. L.25 d 5.3 |
| | 8th " | | In billets at CANAL BANK. Training carried out under Company arrangements. Lieut-Col J KNOTT DSO joined the Batt. and took over Command from Capt J COLHOUN MC who took over duties of Second-in-Command. | do |
| | 9/10" | | In billets at CANAL BANK. Training carried out under Company arrangements. Draft of 64 Other Ranks joined Batt. on 10th inst. | do |

# WAR DIARY
## INTELLIGENCE SUMMARY.
*(Erase heading not required.)*

Army Form C. 2118.

| Place | Date 1918 | Hour | Summary of Events and Information | Remarks and references to Appendices |
|---|---|---|---|---|
| | 11th Ap. | | In billets at CANAL BANK. Training carried out under Company arrangements. The Commanding Officer, Second-in-Command, One Officer per Coy, Signal Officer & Intelligence Officer proceeded to reconnoitre Sector about to be taken over. | BELGIUM 28 N.W. |
| | 12/13th | | Battalion marched to ESSEX FARM and entrained on Light Railway for the Line. – Detrained at BROOKLYN. Coys marched to Line. H.Q Coy at HUBNER FARM. – "A" Coy at WINCHESTER FARM. B & C Coy at BURNS HOUSE and D Coy at OXFORD HOUSE. 10th Royal West Kents on the RIGHT and 1st R.Inniskilling Fusilrs on the LEFT. | ESSEX 28 N.W. ? |
| | 13th | | In the Line. Very little aerial activity owing to mist also very little Artillery Activity. | |
| | 14th | | Some enemy artillery activity, otherwise quiet. Very little aerial | |

# WAR DIARY or INTELLIGENCE SUMMARY.

Army Form C. 2118.

(Erase heading not required.)

| Place | Date | Hour | Summary of Events and Information | Remarks and references to Appendices |
|---|---|---|---|---|
| | 1918 | | | |
| | 14th | AM | activity. Preparations commenced for withdrawal on the night of 15/16" inst. Material which might be of use to the enemy was collected for sending back. Capt J. COLHOUN M.C. took over Command of Battalion Lt Col J.B. KNOTT D.S.O having gone to take over Command of 109th Infantry Brigade, vice Brigadier General HESSEY, D.S.O sick. | |
| | 15th | | Quiet during day. | |
| | 15/16" | | Under orders from 109th Brigade the battalion withdrew from the Outpost line. The night was very dark and the operation was carried out successfully without any interruption from the enemy who were evidently unaware of what was going on. The evacuation commenced about 9.30 p.m. The Outpost Platoon vacated their positions at 4 am. 16th inst bringing with them all the remaining S.A.A., Signals &c and at | |

Army Form C. 2118.

# WAR DIARY
## or
## INTELLIGENCE SUMMARY.
(Erase heading not required.)

| Place | Date | Hour | Summary of Events and Information | Remarks and references to Appendices |
|---|---|---|---|---|
| | 15/16th Apl 1918 | | | BELGIUM Sheet 28 N.W. |
| | | 5.30 am. | the last platoon passed Battn HQ (HUBNER FARM) | |
| | | | Battn HQ moved at 5.45 am and crossed the line on | |
| | | | the banks of the STEENBEEK about an hour later | |
| | | | The platoons on their way from the Outpost Line damaged | |
| | | | as much as possible the duckboard tracks and the | |
| | | | Royal Engineers demolished the Gill Bozes and the | |
| | | | bridges after the troops had withdrawn | |
| | | | Battn having crossed the new Outpost Line marched | CAM 2.23.4 B.3 2.23.4 |
| | | | into billets at CANAL BANK. | |
| | | | An Observing party consisting of 2/Lt ER BERRETT | |
| | | | Sgt Hopkins and 4 Other Ranks was left behind in a | |
| | | | Cul-de-sac just in rear of Bn to observe the | |
| | | | movements of the enemy whom he found out that was | |
| | | | had withdrawn. This party was in Signal Communication | |
| | | | with Brigade HQ with whom they kept in touch with during | |
| | | | the 16th inst. — The enemy put down a heavy barrage | |

Army Form C. 2118.

# WAR DIARY
## or
## INTELLIGENCE SUMMARY.
(Erase heading not required.)

| Place | Date 1918 | Hour | Summary of Events and Information | Remarks and references to Appendices |
|---|---|---|---|---|
| | 15/16th | On the morning of the 16th inst. and continuously on our old line advanced behind it. Lieut. Barrett remained in his position until the German forward patrols were closely approaching and in accordance with his orders he then withdrew without learning or engaged in a fire fight. The party was heavily shelled as they come down the duckboard track (ALBERTA TRACK) and one other rank was killed — the only casualty the Batt. sustained during the operation. | BELGIUM Sheet 28 & 10 |
| | 16th | | Men rested today in their dugouts in the CANAL BANK and with a feet inspections were carried out during the afternoon Enemy Artillery did some shelling on the roads in the neighbourhood of the CANAL BANK | B.14.33 to 14.6.2 |
| | 17th " | | "B" "C" & "D" Coys were engaged in Salvage Work under RE in forward area and "A" Coy were under the orders of Artillery for carrying Ammunition. "B" Coy was recalled during afternoon to Stand by for loading lorryboxes which was later carried out by half - | |

# WAR DIARY
## INTELLIGENCE SUMMARY

Army Form C. 2118.

| Place | Date | Hour | Summary of Events and Information | Remarks and references to Appendices |
|---|---|---|---|---|
| | 17th | 7.30pm | Commence in two reliefs – the second relief being out until 3 am on 18th inst. | BEZ.9104 31.u.28.N.W. |
| | 18th | | "A" & "D" Coys were under orders of the R.E. for railway work. | |
| | | | "C" Coy proceeded at 4 am to be working in the forward area and returned on completion about 9.30 am. "B" Coy was again engaged by half Coys during afternoon – night of 18/19th in loading gravel. 2nd Relief returning about 4 am "B", "C", "D" Coys were employed under R.E. in repairing CANAL defences | |
| | 19th | 8.30pm | Both vacated the billets in CANAL BANK and marched to Brigade support and IRISH FARM Relief complete about 9.45 pm. On completion of relief Batt: "Stood to" for their Battle positions and the C.O. (Capt: J Colhoun M.C.) and Coy Commanders visited all the posts. A Coy Right front, B Coy left front, C Coy Right Support, D Coy left support. | IRISH F'M 31.u.3.6. |

Army Form C. 2118.

# WAR DIARY
## INTELLIGENCE SUMMARY.
*(Erase heading not required.)*

| Place | Date 1918 | Hour | Summary of Events and Information | Remarks and references to Appendices |
|---|---|---|---|---|
| BELGIUM Sh.28NW. C.27.a.3.6. | 19th Apl. | | In billets at IRISH FARM. Considerable enemy Aerial activity from 8.30 p.m. until 10.30 p.m., but no bombs were dropped in Camp. Lieut-Col. R. KNOTT D.S.O. rejoined from 109th Infy Brigade and took over Command | |
| | 20th | | Companies on work in their own area in Battle Zone. Considerable Enemy Aerial Activity at night | |
| | 21st | | Coys on work as for 20th inst. Considerable Enemy Aerial Activity during day, otherwise quiet. | |
| | 22nd | | Our Artillery shelled the enemy sectors on the flanks of our sectors from 4 am until 5 am without any reply from the enemy | |
| | 23rd | | Work as on previous days | |

Army Form C. 2118.

# WAR DIARY
## of
## INTELLIGENCE SUMMARY.
(Erase heading not required.)

Instructions regarding War Diaries and Intelligence Summaries are contained in F. S. Regs., Part II. and the Staff Manual respectively. Title pages will be prepared in manuscript.

| Place | Date 1916 | Hour | Summary of Events and Information | Remarks and references to Appendices |
|---|---|---|---|---|
| | 24th April | | Quiet day. Baths were improvised in Camp and practically the whole Batn was bathed before leaving Reserve | BELGIUM Sheet 28 N.W. |
| | 25th " | | Very heavy bombardment some distance on our Right from 3 am until 8 am. Occasional shelling during the day on roads and tracks. | |
| | 25/26th " | | Batn left IRISH FARM and relieved the 1st Royal Innishilling Fus at WIELTJE. Batn left IRISH FARM about 9.30 pm and relief was complete about 12 midnight. Our line of resistance was behind the STEENBEEK with two Outpost Platoons in front of it. The 107th Bde of 36th Divs was on our left and the 123rd Bde, 41st Divn on our Right. An Boundaries of our front line were at ..... | IRISH FARM G.27.a.7.4. WIELTJE C.23.b.8.5.2. |
| | 26th " 27th " | | Under orders from Brigade the Outpost guns withdrew to the line MOUSE TRAP – PICKLEHAUBE. The Outpost Platoons East of the | C.22.2.7 |

# WAR DIARY
## INTELLIGENCE SUMMARY
*(Erase heading not required.)*

Army Form C. 2118.

| Place | Date 1918 | Hour | Summary of Events and Information | Remarks and references to Appendices |
|---|---|---|---|---|
| BELGIUM | 26/27 | 10 p.m. | STEENBEEK withdrew after dark and the withdrawal of the whole line was complete at 4.30 a.m. 27th inst. This was effected without any interference from the enemy, but their patrols came forward very quickly and were in view of our post before 9 a.m. Our platoons which were on Outpost duty in BOSSAERT and CHEDDAR had to withdraw at 9.30 a.m. 27th inst. as they were nearly surrounded but they inflicted severe casualties on the advancing enemy before they evacuated. Both HQ and | Sh.28 N.E.¼ C.23.b.1.3 C.17.c.4.0 |
| | | | | Our new front line extended from C.22.b.6.6 to C.23.c.5.7 |
| | 27th | 4 p.m. | Coy. remained at WIELTJE. One of the enemy crossed our lines and was taken prisoner. 5th Rgt. Except for occasional shelling the night was fairly quiet. | C.23.c.3.4 |
| | 28th | | The enemy shelled PICKLEHAUBE and WIELTJE very heavily several times during the day. One enemy of the 33rd LANDWEHR Rgt. Prisoner and three of the 33rd were taken prisoners by our advanced posts about 8 p.m. Patrols were sent out frequently and gained | PICKLEHAUBE C.23 |

# WAR DIARY
## INTELLIGENCE SUMMARY.
*(Erase heading not required.)*

Army Form C. 2118.

Instructions regarding War Diaries and Intelligence Summaries are contained in F.S. Regs., Part II. and the Staff Manual respectively. Title pages will be prepared in manuscript.

| Place | Date | Hour | Summary of Events and Information | Remarks and references to Appendices |
|---|---|---|---|---|
| | 1915 28th | am | valuable information. Lieut ROURKE was in charge of one of these patrols and was successful in capturing a prisoner. | BELGIUM Sheet 28 N.W. |
| | 29th | | Batt HQrs moved from WIELTJE to HILLTOP during the afternoon. The enemy again shelled WIELTJE very heavily causing some casualties in the Company which was occupying the line there. Our Artillery put down a very successful barrage between 4am and 5am on the enemy. Patrols were again sent out at night. One Coy of 1st Bn. Roy. Innis. Fus. was attached to this unit at 4 am on 30th and took up reserve position at IRISH FM. | HILL TOP C 21 d 3.7 |
| | 30th | | Enemy again shelled WIELTJE very heavily. Batt was relieved by the 9th Rs Fus. two Relief completed about 12.30 am on 1st May – Batt marched to BRIELEN. Total Casualties during tour — 12 killed + 2 died of wounds and 17 wounded | B 28 + 34 |

Must
Lieut Colonel
Comdg 2nd Royal Inniskilling Fusiliers

2ND ROYAL INNISKILLING FUSILIERS.

Vol. 46

WAR DIARY

FOR MONTH OF MAY, 1918.

Army Form C. 2118.

# WAR DIARY
# INTELLIGENCE SUMMARY. 2nd Bn. Royal Inniskilling Fus.

*(Erase heading not required.)*

Instructions regarding War Diaries and Intelligence Summaries are contained in F.S. Regs., Part II. and the Staff Manual respectively. Title pages will be prepared in manuscript.

| Place | Date 1918 | Hour | Summary of Events and Information | Remarks and references to Appendices |
|---|---|---|---|---|
| BRIELEN | MAY 1st | | Battalion in billets in BRIELEN (B.29) A/gh in CHATEAU at TROIS TOURS (B.28.a.) Batt'n rested during forenoon. Defences of BRIELEN reconnoitred by Commanding Officer and Coy Officers in the afternoon. | Or. |
| " | " 2nd | | Battalion engaged in training and improving defences of BRIELEN during the day. Commanding Officer and Company Commanders reconnoitred the line known as the GREEN LINE (BELGIUM Sheet 28 N.W. B.20. a. and d.) B.26. b. and d. B.27.c. H3. a and c.) A few shells fell during the afternoon in BRIELEN | Or. |
| " | " 3rd | | Training and work continued. 2/Lt. D.J MORIARTY reported the Batt'n today and 2/Lt. G. LODGE joined the Bn from hospital having previously been with the 11th Bn Royal Inns Fus. A draft of 116 Other Ranks joined the Batt'n chiefly from the South Roscommons | Or. |
| " | " 4th | | Training and work continued | Or. |

# WAR DIARY
## INTELLIGENCE SUMMARY.
2nd Bn. Royal Inniskilling Fus

Army Form C. 2118.

*(Erase heading not required.)*

| Place | Date | Hour | Summary of Events and Information | Remarks and references to Appendices |
|---|---|---|---|---|
| BRIELEN | MAY 5 1918 | | Training and work continued in the forenoon - Church Services in the afternoon | (1) |
| " | | 5/6th | At 8pm the Battalion vacated the billets in BRIELEN and took over the CANAL BANK Defences from C.25.a. 80.70. to C.25.d.4.3. - two companies on the EAST Bank and one Coy on the WEST Bank. One Coy of the 9th R. Innis. Fus was also on the WEST Bank under orders of our Commanding Officer. 'B' Coy relieved a Coy of the 1st R. Innis Fus holding a Support line at IRISH FARM (C.28.a. - C.28.c.) Batt. on our right in CANAL BANK was 2nd Royal Irish Rifles, 107th Bde. 36th Division. our left was 12th East Surreys, 41st Division. | (2) |
| CANAL BK | " 6th | | Companies were engaged on Salvage work and improvement of CANAL Defences. Some desultory enemy artillery activity on WEST Bank of CANAL. B Coy vacated the dugouts CANAL Bank and took up a Reserve position at IRISH FARM and came under orders of 1st Bn Royal Innis Fus. | (3) |

Army Form C. 2118.

# WAR DIARY
## INTELLIGENCE SUMMARY.
2nd Royal Inniskilling Fus.

(Erase heading not required.)

Instructions regarding War Diaries and Intelligence Summaries are contained in F.S. Regs., Part II. and the Staff Manual respectively. Title pages will be prepared in manuscript.

| Place | Date 1918 | Hour | Summary of Events and Information | Remarks and references to Appendices |
|---|---|---|---|---|
| CANAL Bk. | 7/5/17 | 7ᵗʰ | Work as on the 6ᵗʰ inst. Enemy carried out considerable counter battery work on batteries behind WEST Bank of CANAL | (1) |
| " | 8ᵗʰ | | Work as on the 6ᵗʰ inst. Day quiet | (2) |
| " | 9ᵗʰ | | Work during forenoon. | (3) |
| " | 9/10ᵗʰ | | All arrangements were made for relieving the 1ˢᵗ Bn Royal Innis Fus in the Line on night of 9/10ᵗʰ inst. but the order/ was cancelled and preparation made for relieving the 23ʳᵈ Middlesex Regt in the Sector on our Right on the night of 10/11ᵗʰ inst. Advance parties went up to Coys of the 23ʳᵈ Bn Middlesex Regt to take over and stayed there over the relief. Salvage work continued today | (4) (5) |
| " | 10ᵗʰ | | Relieved the 23ʳᵈ Middlesex Regt, 132ⁿᵈ Bde, 41ˢᵗ Divn. Relief was completed about 12.30 am on 11ᵗʰ inst. The 15ᵗʰ Hampshire Regt. was on our Right and the 2ⁿᵈ R. Innis. Fus on 107ᵗʰ Bde. | |
| | 19/11 | | H¹⁵ Divn was on our Right and the 2ⁿᵈ R. Innis Fus on 107ᵗʰ Bde 36ᵗʰ Divn on our Left. Our line ran from C28 b 7.4 (left of WIELTJE) to I4 a 9.2 — Batt H.Qrs I3 a.6.7. | (6) |

Army Form C. 2118.

# WAR DIARY
## or
## INTELLIGENCE SUMMARY.  2nd Bn. Royal Inniskilling Fus
*(Erase heading not required.)*

| Place | Date 1918 | Hour | Summary of Events and Information | Remarks and references to Appendices |
|---|---|---|---|---|
| | 9/9/18 | | | |
| | | 10/11° | No movement whatever could be made during the day forward of Batt H.Q. The breastworks were very poor having no parados and were all under direct observation by the enemy. | |
| | " 11th | | Considerable Artillery activity on both sides all day. Very little Aerial Activity | (i) |
| | " 12th | | Considerable Artillery activity all day. Our guns carried out harassing fire on strong points behind the enemy lines. Considerable aerial activity. | (i) |
| | " 13th | | Normal day in sector | (i)(i) |
| | " 14th | | Considerable artillery activity in the afternoon. Enemy gas shelled the neighbourhood of YPRES heavily. | (i) |
| | " 14/15th | | Battalion was relieved night of 14/15 by the 9th Bn. R.Innis.Fus. and moved into reserve at BRIELEN. H.Qrs in CHATEAU TROIS TOURS. The relief was complete about 1 am but the Batt was not settled in billets before 3 am. Casualties during tour 2 Officers | (i) |

# WAR DIARY
## INTELLIGENCE SUMMARY.

2nd Bn. Royal Inniskilling Fus.

Army Form C. 2118.

| Place | Date 1918 | Hour | Summary of Events and Information | Remarks and references to Appendices |
|---|---|---|---|---|
| | MAY 15 | | Wounded (2/Lt. KEOGH and 2nd Lt. SHARPLEY) 2 Other Ranks Killed and 6 Other Ranks wounded. | B |
| BRIELEN | 15 | | Both resting, bathing and cleaning up. | C |
| | | | Coln Rangers attd, joined today for duty. 2/Lt J BYRNE | C |
| " | 16 | | Battalion training | |
| " | 17 | | Half the Battalion training, remainder working under R.E. on BRIELEN defences. On 16th and 17th met the Divisional Concert Troupe "MERRY MAUVES" performed for the benefit of the Battalion - the first evening in SIEGE CAMP and the second evening in CHATEAU TROIS TOURS. The opportunities for bathing afforded by the moat around the Chateau was taken advantage of by all ranks during the tour in BRIELEN. | |
| " | 18 | | Half Battalion training & remainder working under R.E. during forenoon. Church Service in the afternoon | D |

# WAR DIARY
## INTELLIGENCE SUMMARY.
2nd Bn Royal Inniskilling Fus

Army Form C. 2118.

| Place | Date | Hour | Summary of Events and Information | Remarks and references to Appendices |
|---|---|---|---|---|
| | 1918 May 18/19th | | Battalion relieved the 1st Bn Royal Inniskilling Fus on CANAL BANK (Support) One Company being at Wilson's Fm and another at IRISH FARM (C.27.a). Two Companies at CANAL BANK (C.25.d.4.6 to 18.a.4.7) The 23rd Middlesex Regt on our Right (122nd Bde 41st Divn) and on our Left the 9th Royal Irish Fus 108th Bde 36th Divn. Trenches and accommodation fairly good. Desultory enemy artillery activity on roads and bridges over CANAL. Coys working on Defences. | (App 6) |
| | " 19th | | Companies working on Defences. "DEAD END" + vicinity heavily shelled by H.E. between 12 noon and 2 pm. Three enemy aircraft over CANAL about 2pm, they were driven off by our Anti Aircraft guns. | (C) |
| | " 20th | | | (C) |
| | " 21st | | Companies working on Defences. Artillery on both sides very quiet. | (C) (C) |

# WAR DIARY
## INTELLIGENCE SUMMARY. 2nd Royal Inniskilling Fus

Army Form C. 2118.

*(Erase heading not required.)*

| Place | Date | Hour | Summary of Events and Information | Remarks and references to Appendices |
|---|---|---|---|---|
| CANAL BK | 1918 May 22nd | | Companies working on Defences. Batt Hqrs shelled by enemy about 11 am. One shell dropping quite close to the Mess causing considerable damage. No casualties occurred | (1) |
| | 22/23rd | | Battalion relieved the 1st Berks Fus in the line. Disposition of Coys same as in the line from 11th – 14th inst. 12th Royal Irish Rifles 108th Bde on the left – 10th Royal West Kents Regt. 123rd Bde 41st Divn on the Right. | (2) |
| | "23rd" | | Quiet all day with the exception of a few shells which fell near Batt HQ about 9 am. Four Enemy Aircraft over our lines about 9 am. | (3) |
| | "24th" | | Front line heavily bombarded with T.M shells early in the morning. Very quiet all day. Rain fell during day preventing aerial activity. | (4) |
| | "25th" | | Bombardment of our front line resumed this morning. Very quiet all day. One Enemy Aircraft over our line about noon | (5) |

Army Form C. 2118.

# WAR DIARY
## of
## INTELLIGENCE SUMMARY. 2nd Royal Inniskilling Fus

(Erase heading not required.)

| Place | Date | Hour | Summary of Events and Information | Remarks and references to Appendices |
|---|---|---|---|---|
| | 1918 MAY 26" | | Very quiet all day | |
| | 26/27" | | The Battalion was relieved by the 9th Rhine Fus and moved into Reserve at BRIELEN. The relief was complete about 12 midnight. – Casualties during tour 1 Officer wounded 2/Lieut BOGLE and 1 OR Killed, 8 ORanks wounded | |
| BRIELEN | "27" | | From 12.30 a.m. to about 4 a.m. the enemy shelled the area very heavily with H.E. and gas shells paying particular attention to the Batteries. The Companies were delayed in getting to BRIELEN but except for a few who went gassed the Casualties were slight. | |
| | "28 | | Battalion billeted at BRIELEN. Working parties consisting of two Coys working under R.E. on BRIELEN Line. Remaining two Coys training | |
| | "29 | | Companies on Working Parties & training as on 28" inst. Enemy Artillery shelled very heavily in the vicinity of the CHATEAU TROIS TOURS suddenly searching for our Batteries which | |

# WAR DIARY
## INTELLIGENCE SUMMARY. 2nd Royal Inniskilling Fus

Army Form C. 2118.

(Erase heading not required.)

| Place | Date 1918 MAY | Hour | Summary of Events and Information | Remarks and references to Appendices |
|---|---|---|---|---|
| BRIELEN. | 29 | | were very active during the day | |
| " | 30 | | Battalion employed as on the 28th & 29th | |
| " | 30/31st | | Battalion relieved the 1st Royal Innis Fus at CANAL BANK. KAAIE Defences - A Coy at WILSON FM (C.26.b) B Coy KAAIE Defences - C Coy IRISH FM (C.27.a) D Coy at CANAL BANK. | |

21.5.18.

M Austin
Lt Col
Comdg 2nd R. Innis Fus

— Confidential —

War Diary

of

2nd Bn. Royal Inniskilling Fusrs

From 1st June 1918    To 30th June, 1918

(Volume 47).

Army Form C. 2118.

# WAR DIARY
## of
## INTELLIGENCE SUMMARY. 2nd Royal Inniskilling Fusiliers

*(Erase heading not required.)*

Instructions regarding War Diaries and Intelligence Summaries are contained in F. S. Regs., Part II. and the Staff Manual respectively. Title pages will be prepared in manuscript.

Vol 47

| Place | Date 1918 | Hour | Summary of Events and Information | Remarks and references to Appendices |
|---|---|---|---|---|
| Sheet 28 N.W. | June 1st | | In Brigade Support at CANAL BANK. Dispositions of Companies:- <br> A. Coy - WILSON'S FARM (C26.b.72) <br> B. " - KAAIE DEFENCES (C12.c.82) <br> C. " - IRISH FARM. (C27.a.26) <br> D. " - CANAL BANK. " <br> H'qrs - " (I.l.86) | |
| Sheet 27. | 3/4th | | "B" and "D" Coys were employed on Salvage work. Battalion relieved by 1st Battalion of the 2nd Grenadier Regiment, 12th Division (Belgian Army), and moved by train to PROVEN ASH STATION thence by route march to TUNNELLING CAMP and came in to II Corps Reserve. - Time of arrival at latter place about 5 a.m. | F27 a 48 |
| | 5th | | Remainder of day the Battalion was resting. Day devoted to cleaning up and inspections by Company Commanders | |
| | 6th | | Commanding Officer inspected the Battalion which was formed up in Mass on Parade Ground After the inspection, Companies carried out training | |

Army Form C. 2118.

# WAR DIARY
# ~~INTELLIGENCE~~ SUMMARY.
*(Erase heading not required.)*

2nd Royal Innuskilling Fusrs

| Place | Date | Hour | Summary of Events and Information | Remarks and references to Appendices |
|---|---|---|---|---|
| TUNNELLING CAMP | June 7/8 1918 | 9th | Training of Companies and Specialists. Sunday - Divine Services. Remainder of day spent in Recreation, etc. | W. |
| " | " | 10th | Sports were arranged by the Battalion. After a good programme which was enjoyed by all ranks the Prizes were distributed by Brig-General W.F.HESSEY, D.S.O. to the various winners. | W. W. |
| " | " 10/11th | | Training of Companies and Specialists. | |
| " | " 12th | | Battalion moved to Musketry Camps to carry out training. - Headquarters, "A" & "B" Coys by route march to MOME HOUCK near CASSEL "C" and "D" Coys under command of Major J. COLHOUN, M.C., entrained at WATOU, and detrained at BOLZEELE, thence by route march to RUBRUCK Area and billeted. Transport and other details remained at TUNNELLING CAMP. | P.8. c.46 H.2.c.24 & 17.6.68. |
| " | " 13/16th | | Musketry Practices carried out by all ranks. | F27 a.48 W. W. |

# WAR DIARY
## INTELLIGENCE SUMMARY.

2nd Royal Inniskilling Fusiliers

Army Form C. 2118.

| Place | Date 1918 | Hour | Summary of Events and Information | Remarks and references to Appendices |
|---|---|---|---|---|
| TUNNELLING CAMP. | Jun. 16th | | Battalion returned to TUNNELLING CAMP. | |
| " | " 17th | | Companies placed at disposal of Company Commanders | |
| " | " 18th | | Commanding Officers inspection – Battalion formed up in Mass on Parade Ground. | |
| " | " 19/20th | | Training of Companies also Specialists | |
| " | " 21st | | Battalion relieved by the 2nd Royal Irish Rifles and marched to PETERBOROUGH CAMP, PROVEN AREA, Fr. d. 25 and was in Brigade Reserve | |
| PETERBORO' CAMP. | " 21/29th | | Companies found Working Parties of 105 Other Ranks each, for work on the EAST POPERINGHE Line, under CRE | |
| " | " 23rd + 28th | | Also found a Working Party of 100 other Ranks for work on Battery Positions, under C.R.A. The C.R.A. thanked the 109th Brigade for the good work done on the Battery Positions. | |

Army Form C. 2118.

# WAR DIARY
## INTELLIGENCE SUMMARY.

2nd Royal Inniskilling Fusiliers

(Erase heading not required.)

| Place | Date | Hour | Summary of Events and Information | Remarks and references to Appendices |
|---|---|---|---|---|
| | 1918 Jun. 30th | | Battalion relieved by the 9th Royal Irish Fusiliers 108th Brigade. Transport, staff and details marched to Bois St. ACAIRE. Companies after completion of work on the EAST POPERINGHE Line entrained for PUGWASH STN. thence by route march to BOIS ST. ACAIRE. Lewis Gunners of the Battalion moved to Muckethy Camp at CASSEL for firing practice and formed part of the 109th Bde Lewis Gun Detachment under command of Major E.N. CRAWFORD, D.S.O., 9th Bn. Royal Inniskilling Fus. | D.20.d.65 |
| " | | | | |

M. Neill
Lieut-Col.
Commdg 2nd R. Inniskilling Fus.

— Confidential —

## War Diary

of

"2nd" Battalion Royal Inniskilling Fusiliers

From 1st July 1918    To 31st July 1918

( Volume 48 )

*[signature]* Lieut-Col
Comdg 2" Ry Inniskilling Fus

# WAR DIARY
## INTELLIGENCE SUMMARY.
2nd Bn. Royal Inniskilling Fus.

Army Form C. 2118.

| Place | Date 1918 | Hour | Summary of Events and Information | Remarks and references to Appendices |
|---|---|---|---|---|
| | July 1st/2nd | | Battalion encamped at BOIS ST ACAIRE. Coys at disposal of Company Commanders for Section training &c. Also training of Specialists carried out. | |
| | " 3rd | 3.30 | The 109th Infantry Brigade moved to Reserve XVI French Corps Area, and came under that Corps for tactical purposes. Battalion moved by route march to BAVINCHOVE (OXELAERE Area, Sheet 27 Ed. 3. (O.17) and billeted. — ROUTE:- WINNEZEELE – RWELD – O.12.b.4.4 – OXELAERE. The Lewis Gun Detachment at CASSEL rejoined Battalion at BAVINCHOVE, where Batn HQrs and three Companies were billeted, — one Coy was billeted in TROIS ROIS. | |
| | " 4th-6th | | Companies at disposal of O's. C. Companies — organisation & training of Specialists. | |
| | " 7/8th | | Battalion moved into forward area and was in Divisional | |

Army Form C. 2118.

# WAR DIARY
## or
## INTELLIGENCE SUMMARY. 2nd Bn Royal Inniskilling Fusrs

(Erase heading not required.)

| Place | Date 1918 | Hour | Summary of Events and Information | Remarks and references to Appendices |
|---|---|---|---|---|
| | July 7th | | Reserve, relieving the 23rd Bn. d'Infanterie (French) Sheet 27 S.E. & 28 S.W. Dispositions of Companies as follows:— | |
| | | | Battn H'qrs  - BOESCHEPE. (R.10.a.23) | |
| | | | "A" Coy    - Mt KOKEREELE. (R.17.c.31). | |
| | | | "B"  "      - LE PURGATOIRE } (R.23.b.78). | |
| | | | "C"  "        STAINER HOUSE } | |
| | | | "D"  "      - LOUI FARM. (R.10.d.72) | |
| | | | for Counter-attack purposes. | |
| | | | Transport remained behind at CAESTRE. Details at BAVINCHOVE (Sheet 27. O.17.) under Command of Capt. A.C. LENDRUM, M.C. | A. |
| | "8/10th" | | Battalion in billets as above. A few enemy H.E. shells fired into village occupied by Batn. H'qrs (BOESCHEPE). | B. |
| | "11/14th" | | Enemy again shelled the village of BOESCHEPE. Companies out on working Parties under R.E. on the ERMITAGE - LA MANCHE Line at night P.35.b. P.36.a | C. |
| | "16th" | | "D" Coy moved to Mt NOIR and come under the Command of Major SMITH M.C. for garrison of Mt NOIR. | D. |

Army Form C. 2118.

# WAR DIARY
# INTELLIGENCE SUMMARY. 2nd Bn Royal Inniskilling Fusiliers

(Erase heading not required.)

| Place | Date | Hour | Summary of Events and Information | Remarks and references to Appendices |
|---|---|---|---|---|
| | July 14/18 | | Companies on Working Parties under R.E.s | |
| | " 19th | | Hostile Shelling of the village of BOESCHEPE from about 9am to 9.30 am. "D" Coy was relieved by No 2 Coy "16th" Royal Irish Rifles (P.) at MT NOIR and took over billets as previously occupied by them. | (A) |
| | " 20/22nd | | Two Companies on Working Parties under R.E. and two Companies Training, which was carried out at night. | (B) |
| | " 22/23rd | | Battalion moved into trenches and relieved 1st Royal Irish Fusiliers, in the Left Subsector of ST JANS CAPPEL Sector — On the left 18th/18th Highland Light Infantry Bde 25th Division and on the Right 9th Bn R. Innis Fus, 109th Infy Bde. Dispositions of Companies:— "B" Coy — Left front   "A" Coy — Right front "C"   "  — Support       "D" —       Reserve Batt. Hqtrs at M. 33. b. 30. | (C) |

Army Form C. 2118.

# WAR DIARY
## of
## INTELLIGENCE SUMMARY.
(Erase heading not required.)

2nd Bn Royal Inniskilling Fus

| Place | Date 1918 | Hour | Summary of Events and Information | Remarks and references to Appendices |
|---|---|---|---|---|
| | July 22/23rd | | En route to the trenches Battalion was subjected to a bombardment of "Yellow Cross" Shells, and H.E's. | A. B. |
| | 23/26th | | In Trenches. | |
| | 27/28th | | Battalion relieved in the line by the 1st Royal Inniskilling Fus. and withdrew to M.19.d.7.0 and were in Brigade Reserve. Casualties during tour in the line – 2 Other Ranks Killed. 8 Other Ranks wounded, and 22 Other Ranks gassed. | B. |
| | 28/31st | | In Brigade Reserve :–<br>Bn. H.Qrs. at M.19.d.7.0<br>A Coy " " M.19.d.3.3<br>B " " " M.20.c.2.1<br>C " " " M.26.a.5.9<br>D " " " M.25.d.7.8<br>30 O.Ranks working under R.E. Tunnellers in course of construction through Mt Kemmel.<br>Working parties mainly for work under R.E. | Sheet 28 S.W. 1/20000<br>Ed 7B. Local<br>B. |

Army Form C. 2118.

# WAR DIARY
# INTELLIGENCE SUMMARY.   2nd Royal Inniskilling Fusiliers

(Erase heading not required.)

| Place | Date | Hour | Summary of Events and Information | Remarks and references to Appendices |
|---|---|---|---|---|
| | July 31 / 1st Aug 1918 | | Battalion relieved 9th Bn Royal Inniskilling Fusiliers in the Right Sub. Sector of the 109th Infy Brigade Sector. - 1st Bn Royal Innis Fus. on the left and 15th Ry Irish Rifles 107th Brigade, 36th Division, on the Right. - Dispositions of Companies:-<br>D Coy - Left Front   C. Coy - Right Front<br>A " - Support        B " - Reserve<br>B/Hqrs at M.32.a.0.1. | |

M[signature]
Lieut-Colonel
Comdg 2nd Royal Inniskilling Fusiliers

War Diary.

Volume 48.

August 1918.

2nd Bn. Royal Inniskilling Fusiliers.

Army Form C. 2118.

# WAR DIARY
## INTELLIGENCE SUMMARY.
2nd Bn. Rl. Inniskilling Fusiliers

(Erase heading not required.)

Instructions regarding War Diaries and Intelligence Summaries are contained in F. S. Regs., Part II. and the Staff Manual respectively. Title pages will be prepared in manuscript.

| Place | Date 1918 | Hour | Summary of Events and Information | Remarks and references to Appendices |
|---|---|---|---|---|
| | August 1st | | On the night of the 1st about 11 p.m. an officers Patrol under command of Capt. J.L. Hardy "B" Coy went out to reconnoitre SHODDY FM. S 8 a 75. On reaching their objective they came in contact with the enemy who opened M.G. fire and threw some bombs at the Patrol wounding Capt. Hardy. No 9432 Sgt Gaynor Capt Hardy shot one of the enemy the remainder took flight, still attacked by M.G. fire he ordered his party back to our own trenches remaining with Sgt. Gaynor who was severely wounded whom he dragged to about 200 yards to a place of safety and went to where he reached our lines. | G.2.H. G.2.H. |
| Do | 2/3rd | | In trenches | |
| Do | 4/5 | | Inter. coy. relief. Disposition of companies — "B" Coy. - Left Front "C" Coy Support "A" " Right Front "D" " Reserve | |
| | | | On our Right 12th ROYAL IRISH RIFLES. On our Left 1st ROYAL INNISKILLING FUS. | G.2.H. G.2.H. |
| Do | 6/8th | | In trenches. | G.2.H. |
| Do | 8/9th | | Relieved by the 9th Rl. Irish Fusiliers and marched to Dud. Reserve | G.2.H. |

**Army Form C. 2118.**

# WAR DIARY
## or
## INTELLIGENCE SUMMARY.
2nd Bn. Rl. Innis killing Fusiliers

(Erase heading not required.)

Instructions regarding War Diaries and Intelligence Summaries are contained in F. S. Regs., Part II. and the Staff Manual respectively. Title pages will be prepared in manuscript.

| Place | Date | Hour | Summary of Events and Information | Remarks and references to Appendices |
|---|---|---|---|---|
| | August | 8/9/17 | (Boeschepe Area) Dispositions of Companies :- | |
| | | | "A" Coy MT KOKEREELE "C" Coy LOUI FARM | |
| | | | "B" " SUTTON FARM "D" " LOUI FARM | 9.2.M. |
| | | | Headquarters :- BOSCHEPE | |
| | | | Casualties during tour in line :- 1 Officer wounded 1 O.R. killed | |
| | | | 1 O.R. Died of Wounds 2 O.R. Wounded | |
| | 5t | 9/6/12" | Companies on Working parties under R.E. | |
| | | | B.H.Q (BOSCHEPE) Shelled on the 11th and 12th by the Enemy with H.E. are | 9.2.M. |
| | | | nothing. 6 and almost shrapnel adjoining house – shelling | |
| | | | every five minutes lasted about one hour each day – Casualties | |
| | | | Nunter (Act. Batt.) wounded | |
| | Do | 13th/14th | Companies on Working Parties | 9.2.M. |
| | Do | 15/16/17 | Companies on Working Parties | 9.2.M. |
| | Do | 18th/19th | Three Platoons of "D" Coy proceded to L.29.c.5.8 (M.Shu=27) for work | 9.2.M. |
| | | | under O.C. 76 – 1 Screwaps Company and bivouacked this | |
| | Do | 20" | Remainder of "D" Coy and other two Coys on Working Parties | 9.2.M. |

**Army Form C. 2118.**

# WAR DIARY
## or
## INTELLIGENCE SUMMARY.
*(Erase heading not required.)*

Instructions regarding War Diaries and Intelligence Summaries are contained in F. S. Regs., Part II. and the Staff Manual respectively. Title pages will be prepared in manuscript.

| Place | Date 1918 | Hour | Summary of Events and Information | Remarks and references to Appendices |
|---|---|---|---|---|
| | August 20th | | For conspicuous gallantry whilst in charge of an offensive patrol mentioned in this Diary on 1st August Capt Hardy was awarded the M.C. | 9.2.H. |
| | | | | 9.2.H. |
| | 23rd/24th | | 4 companies on working parties | |
| | 24th/25th | | Battalion moved into trenches and relieved 1st Bn. Rifle Brigade | |
| | | | in the RIGHT sub sector of the ST JANS CAPPEL sector. Disposition of coys:- | 9.2.H. |
| | | | "C" Coy. RIGHT FRONT    "D" Coy. LEFT FRONT | |
| | | | "B"     CENTRE         "A"     SUPPORT | |
| | | | En route to trenches the battalion was subjected to a considerable amount of gas shelling | 9.2.H. |
| | 26th | | In trenches | 9.2.H. |
| | 27th | | In trenches  "B" Coy moved to support | |
| | 28th | | In trenches | 9.2.H. |
| | 29th | | In trenches | |
| | 30th | | Enemy retired  Patrols from C+D Coys followed Battn. advanced to line Sqd 55 - S.15.b.59 + S.15.d.81 - S.15.b.22 Bn. Hqrs at SHODDY FARM. | 9.2.H. |

Army Form C. 2118.

# WAR DIARY
## INTELLIGENCE SUMMARY. 2nd Bn. Rl. Inniskilling Fusiliers
*(Erase heading not required.)*

| Place | Date | Hour | Summary of Events and Information | Remarks and references to Appendices |
|---|---|---|---|---|
| | 1918 August 31 | | Battalion advanced to THORNTON RD S.23a.4.6 - S.23.b.6.6 where it became support to 1st Bn. Rl. Inniskilling Fusiliers who from above point | |
| | | | Battalion Headquarters at WART FARM. | J.J.H. |
| | | | Total casualties during tour | |
| | | | 2 Officers Killed.   3 Officers wounded | |
| | | | 9 Other Ranks killed   54 Other Ranks wounded | J.J.H. |
| | | | 1 Other Ranks missing | |
| | | | | |
| | | | J.J. Hardy Capt. | |
| | | | The Connaught Rangers. | |
| | | | attchd. 2nd R. Inniskilling Fusiliers | |

Confidential

49 H.

War Diary

— of —

2ⁿᵈ Royal Inniskilling Fusiliers

From 1ˢᵗ Sept 1918      To 30ᵗʰ Sept 1918.

— Confidential —

## War Diary

of

2nd Battalion Royal Inniskilling Fusrs

From :- 1st September — To :- 30th September 1918

— Volume 50. —

E.W. Crawford
Major
Comdg 2 R. Innis. Fus.

# WAR DIARY
## INTELLIGENCE SUMMARY. 2nd Bn Royal Inniskilling Fusrs

Army Form C. 2118.

(Erase heading not required.)

| Place | Date 1918 | Hour | Summary of Events and Information | Remarks and references to Appendices |
|---|---|---|---|---|
| | Sept. 1. | | Advance continued as far as HILLSIDE CAMP. | |
| | | | "C" Coy captured an enemy Machine Gun No 41628 Cpl. JONES and two prisoners of the 156 I.R. | |
| | | | Lieut K.C. SANDEMAN 11th Hamps. Regt. attd 2nd R.Innis. Fus. and 2 Lieut MORIARTY | |
| | | | Killed in Action - 2 Lieut Bn Bogh Died of Wounds | |
| | "1-2nd | | Battalion was relieved by 1st Royal Irish Fusiliers and moved to | |
| MAGHEREELE | | | Divisional Reserve (M. KOHEREELE) | |
| | " 2nd | | Battalion resting - Cleaning up etc. | |
| | / 3rd | | Battalion moved to MAGILLIGAN CAMP - Disposition - | |
| | | | Batt H Qrs S.15.k.45.95. "A" Coy S.10.c.g.4. "B" Coy S.10.c.40.15. "C" Coy S.15.k.3.8 Sht° | 28 S.W. 3 |
| | | | "D" Coy. S.10.c.72. | 1:10000 |
| | | H | In Divisional Reserve | |
| | " 5 | | Battalion moved to WATERLOO CAMP - Disposition | |
| | | | Batt H Qrs S.18.c.8.3. "A" S.18.d.5.8. "B" S.18.b.95.15. "C" S.18.a.82. "D". S.18.d.o.2. | |
| | | | Batt Hqts and vicinity shelled by enemy with Gas Shells, | |
| | | | lasting about two hours | |

# WAR DIARY
## INTELLIGENCE SUMMARY.
2nd Bn. Royal Inniskilling Fusrs

Army Form C. 2118.

(Erase heading not required.)

| Place | Date 1918 | Hour | Summary of Events and Information | Remarks and references to Appendices |
|---|---|---|---|---|
| | Sept 6th-7th | | Quiet day with the exception of CRUCIFIX CORNER where Coys were lying which was shelled intermittently by enemy H.V. shells | |
| | " 8th | 3.30 pm | Battalion moved to MAGILLIGAN CAMP to same positions as occupied on 3rd instant | |
| | " 9-15th | | In billets at MAGILLIGAN CAMP. - Coys at disposal of Coy Commanders training +c. | |
| | " 15/16 | | Battalion relieved the 1st Royal Irish Rifles in Reserve Line Dispositions of Coys - "A" Coy T.16.a.60.45. - "B" Coy T.g.d.90.50. - "C" Coy T.16.a.60.80 - "D" Coy T.g.d.90.65. B+to T.16.a 40.45 | SHEET 28 S.W. 1/20,000 |
| | " 16th | | Enemy shelled the area occupied by Battn with H.E + H.Y. shells, many dropping in vicinity of Battn H.Qrs. | |
| | | 3 pm | Continued shelling of area, one H.V. shell bursting at door of H.Qrs. Mess killing Lieut-Col. L. de V. FITZGERALD, who was in Command of Battn. wounding Major G. M. FORDE, D.S.O. Second-in-Command, and Lieut E. M. PHILPS, Intelligence Officer. O'Ranks 1 killed 2 wounded Major A. E. GALLAGHER D.S.O. Munster Fusrs took over command of Battn. but was subsequently relieved by | |

Army Form C. 2118.

# WAR DIARY
## INTELLIGENCE SUMMARY.
*(Erase heading not required.)*

2nd Bn Royal Innskilling Fusrs

| Place | Date 1918 | Hour | Summary of Events and Information | Remarks and references to Appendices |
|---|---|---|---|---|
| | Sept 16 | | Owing to the continued shelling of Batt. H.Qrs, the position was vacated and moved to where "C" Coy was where they dug themselves in. Enemy continued to shell Battn Area during night killing 1 OR wounding 2 ORanks | |
| | " 17-19th | | Battalion still in Reserve at NEUVE EGLISE. Continued shelling of area. | |
| | " 19/20 | | The 2/15th London Regt relieved the 1st + 2nd Battns R Innis Fuslrs in Support and Reserve Lines. - B Coy 2/15th London Regt relieving A + C Coys right half reserve garrison. - "D" " " " B + D Coys left half of reserve garrison. Battalion then marched to ASYLUM Area (BAILLEUL) and billeted there for the night. | |
| | " 20 | 5 pm | Battalion marched to EECKE Area and billeted there | |
| | " 21 - 22nd | | —————ditto————— | |
| | " 22nd | 7.30 pm | Battalion marched from EECKE to WORMHOUDT (C. Sub - Area) and billeted there. | |

# WAR DIARY
## or
## INTELLIGENCE SUMMARY.

2nd Royal Inniskilling Fusrs

Army Form C. 2118.

| Place | Date 1918 | Hour | Summary of Events and Information | Remarks and references to Appendices |
|---|---|---|---|---|
| | Sept 23-24th | | Battalion billeted in WORMHOUDT. | |
| | " 25 | | The Divisional Commander Major-General C.COFFIN, V.C., D.S.O., presented Decorations to the following Officers & Other Ranks of the Battalion for conspicuous gallantry displayed in Action:— | |
| | | | Capt J.C. PATON, M.C., C.F. — Bar to Military Cross | |
| | | | " J.L. HARDY "C" Coy. — Military Cross | |
| | | | C.S.M. G. NEWMAN " — Military Medal | |
| | | | 8612 Sgt. R. McNEILL, M.M. — Bar to Military Medal | |
| | | | 2293 " G. EVANS — Military Medal | |
| | | | 895 Cpl R. KANE, M.M. — Bar to Military Medal | |
| | | | 25363 " R. LUMSDEN — Military Medal | |
| | | | 43575 " F. STRINGER, "C" Coy — do — | |
| | | | 4628 Pte 19 JONES — do — | |
| | | | 2446 Gt A. McDOWELL — do — | |
| | | | The Divisional Commander congratulated the recipients on their well earned distinctions | |
| | " 26th | | Coys at disposal of Coy Commanders. Training &c | |

— Confidential —

# War Diary

of the

2nd. Battalion Royal Inniskilling Fusiliers,

From October 1st, to October 31st, 1918.

## VOLUME 51.

E.W. Crawford.
Lt. Col., Comdg.
2nd. Bn. R. Inniskilling Fus.

Army Form C. 2118.

# WAR DIARY
## or
## INTELLIGENCE SUMMARY.
(Erase heading not required.)

2nd Bn. Royal Inniskilling Fusiliers

109/36 I.

Vol 51

| Place | Date | Hour | Summary of Events and Information | Remarks and references to Appendices |
|---|---|---|---|---|
| REFERENCE MAP SHEET 28 N.E.4. DADIZEELE 1/10,000. | Oct. 1. | 12:00 | The Battalion withdrew into Reserve in squares K15 a and c, but about 12:00 received orders to move up into support to the 1st Bn. R. Inniskilling Fus. who were to attack southwards along the line of the ROULERS-MENIN Railway. "C" Coy. went into immediate support at K12c6045, Battalion H.Q. & the remainder of the Battalion being at PEASE CORNER. However the orders to attack were cancelled and the Battalion proceeded to relieve the 1st Royal Irish Fusiliers and part of the 12th Royal Irish Rifles in the line on the night of the 1st/2nd. Dispositions:- H. Qrs. I24a73; "A" Coy. K18d92 - L13c62; "B" Coy. in reserve at K18c72; "C" Coy. from MONKS FORK to TWIG FARM inclusive; "D" Coy. from K24a73 to K24 b 23 with one platoon in support at K18d86. | 80e. |
| | Oct. 2. | | The post of "C" Coy. at TWIG FARM was this afternoon driven out by an enemy attack under a heavy artillery and Machine Gun barrage but was retaken by a counter attack under CAPT. HARDY, M.C. and a Company of the 9th Bn. immediately afterwards. At this time MAJOR GALLAGHER, D.S.O. and CAPT. HARDY, M.C., were informed. The day ended with fairly | 65c. |

Army Form C. 2118.

# WAR DIARY
## or
## INTELLIGENCE SUMMARY.
(Erase heading not required.)

Instructions regarding War Diaries and Intelligence Summaries are contained in F. S. Regs., Part II. and the Staff Manual respectively. Title pages will be prepared in manuscript.

| Place | Date | Hour | Summary of Events and Information | Remarks and references to Appendices |
|---|---|---|---|---|
| REFERENCE MAP SHEET 28.N.W. 1/20,000. | Oct. 3. | | Heavy enemy shelling and almost complete silence on the part of our artillery. Roads were patrolled from DADIZEELE to TWIG FARM and from PEASE CORNER to VIJFWEGEN. MAJOR E.N.CRAWFORD, D.S.O, 9th Bn. assumed command of the Battn. Fairly heavy shelling all day on our posts, and roads in our area. On the night of the 3rd/4th the Battalion was relieved in the line by the 9th Battalion, and moved back into Brigade Reserve. Dispositions — Battn. H.Q. K.17.b.4.7; "A" Coy. K.11.c.8.0; "B" Coy. K.17.b.4.3; "C" Coy. K.16.b.9.8; "D" Coy. K.11.d.6.5.00. | Eob. |
| | Oct. 4. | | The Battalion remained in Brigade Reserve until the night of the 4th/5th when it was relieved by the 1st Bn. Royal Irish Fusiliers and marched back to billets around K.14.b.6.0. | Eob. |
| | Oct. 5. | | Was spent by the Battalion in resting and cleaning up, etc. | Eob. |
| | Oct. 6. | | The Battalion moved by light railway, entraining at BROODSEINDE, to billets in BRAKE CAMP a portion of DIRTY BUCKET CAMP. A wet night, not improved by minor accidents on the railway. Detraining point HAGLE-Cab central. | Eob. |

Army Form C. 2118.

# WAR DIARY
## or
## INTELLIGENCE SUMMARY
(Erase heading not required.)

2nd R. Inniskilling Fusiliers.

| Place | Date | Hour | Summary of Events and Information | Remarks and references to Appendices |
|---|---|---|---|---|
| | Oct. 7, 8, 9, 10 & 11th. | 1918. | Resting, replenishing battle stores, cleaning up, and training at Brake Camp. On the 11th, orders were received to proceed by light railway to ZONNEBEKE on the following day. | |
| REFERENCE MAP SHEET 28 N.E.4. | Oct. 12. | | The Battalion entrained under MAJOR CRAWFORD, D.S.O., at HAGLE at 15.00, and proceeded by the light railway to ZONNEBEKE, arriving at 18.20, from which place they marched to K 7 & 8, spending the night in bivouacs there. Occasional shells from the enemy dropped unpleasantly close. | |
| | Oct. 13. | | Orders were received from the Battalion to attack on the following morning so the day was spent in completing the issue of battle stores. At 23.15 the Battalion left its billets to march into battle positions. | |
| | Oct. 14. | | 02.00 saw the Battalion in the following positions:— "B" Coy. in close liaison with the left of 1st Battn. at K13 a 62. "C" Coy. on the right at K18 central and K18 d 7085, keeping touch with the left of the 1st Royal Irish Rifles. "D" Coy. on the left from K18 a 15 – K18 a 02, keeping touch with the right | |

# WAR DIARY
## INTELLIGENCE SUMMARY

Army Form C. 2118.

2nd Bn. Royal Inniskilling Fus.

| Place | Date | Summary of Events and Information | Remarks and references to Appendices |
|---|---|---|---|
| | 1918. | of the 4th Worcester Regt. - 29th Division. "A" Coy. in support from K18a 2.8 – K18a 15, having two platoons on either flank, and keeping touch with the 2nd Royal Irish Rifles on the right and the 2nd Bn. Hampshire Regt. on the left. Battalion H.Q. was located at K18a + 0.55.  The enemy shelled the area in which the Battalion lay before Zero hour, fortunately without inflicting any casualties.  Zero hour was at 05.35 and at 05.30 our artillery commenced the barrage fire. At Zero the Battalion followed the 1st Battn. in the attack and "B" Coy. was early called on to fill a gap left by the 1st Battn. who had lost direction somewhat owing to the mist and amount of smoke.  The attack continued and at about 09.30 the Battalion passed through the 1st Battn., having "C" & "D" Coys. in the front line; "A" Coy. in support and "B" Coy. in reserve. Strong opposition was met with, principally from Machine Guns. A battery of four opp. guns, with several Machine Guns | |

Army Form C. 2118.

# WAR DIARY
or
INTELLIGENCE SUMMARY.

2nd R. Inniskilling Fusiliers

| Place | Date | Hour | Summary of Events and Information | Remarks and references to Appendices |
|---|---|---|---|---|
| REFERENCE MAP SHEET 29. | | | was captured at G.13.b.25 by "D" Coy. under CAPT. LENDRUM, M.C. Here the advance was held up somewhat by a burning ammunition dump and accurate shelling, the enemy having good observation from the Church at GULLEGHEM. However, after MAJOR E.W. CRAWFORD, D.S.O. had, ~~with the support of 8 Coy~~, reconnoitred the line, the advance continued, finally ending for the day at G.14.a.5.c central. Letter of congratulation on successes received from the Army Commander. | "etc." |
| | Oct. 15. | | At 01.40 orders were received to continue the advance which re-started at 09.00. Strong belts of wire outside GULLEGHEM held it up somewhat & caused a number of casualties but eventually the village was taken, liberating a large number of civilians thereby. The Battalion reached its final objective id G.22 central, & the 9th Battalion, commanded by Lt. Col. KNOX, D.S.O., passed through & captured the village of HEULE. The 2nd Battn. proceeded to dig in at G.16.c central. A further letter of congratulation received from the Army Commander, the II Corps gaining an special mention. | "etc." |

Army Form C. 2118.

VI.

# WAR DIARY
## or
## INTELLIGENCE SUMMARY.
(Erase heading not required.)

2nd. Royal Inniskilling Fusiliers

| Place | Date 1918. | Summary of Events and Information | Remarks and references to Appendices |
|---|---|---|---|
| | Oct. 16. | The battalion withdrew to billets at LEDEGHEM, being relieved in the line by the 29th. Division. | &c. |
| | Oct. 17. | Spent in cleaning up and refitting. MAJOR-GENERAL COFFIN, V.C., D.S.O., paid a visit to the Battalion and complimented it on the good work done in the advance. | &c. |
| | Oct. 18. | Orders were received to take over part of the line held by the 11th. Regt. Belgian Infantry. The battalion marched from LEDEGHEM at 10.45, through LENDELEDE to HULSTE where they spent an uncomfortable night in billets being shelled with H.E. & gas, & being bombed. | &c. |
| | Oct. 19. | Was spent in cleaning up, etc. Orders received during the day reference the attack across the river LYS and at 21.00 the Battalion moved to B17c84, "B" Coy. being in Liaison with the right of the Belgian Divisions. Dispositions "A" Coy., B17c71; "B" Coy., C14a38; "C" Coy., B23d47; "D" Coy., B17d84; Battn. H.Q., B17a85. | &c. |

Army Form C. 2118.

# WAR DIARY
## or
## INTELLIGENCE SUMMARY.
(Erase heading not required.)

2nd Royal Inniskilling Fusiliers

| Place | Date 1918 | Hour | Summary of Events and Information | Remarks and references to Appendices |
|---|---|---|---|---|
| | Oct. 20. | | "C" Coy. was called on to support the 1st Battn and moved to C.19.d.59 with one platoon at C.14.a.84. No casualties in crossing the river LYS. | etc. |
| | | | Battalion H.Q. moved at 10.00 to B.18.c.95.40; "A" Coy. to B.18.d.78; "D" Coy. to C.13.c.73. "B" & "C" Coys. did not move, but at about 22.00 "C" Coy. were brought back to B.18.d.81, being no longer required by the 1st Battalion. | etc. |
| | Oct. 21. | | "B" Coy. were brought back to more comfortable billets at B.18.d.81, with "C" Coy., as they were no longer necessary on the left flank. | etc. |
| | Oct. 22. | | The Battalion remained in billets. | etc. |
| | Oct. 23. | | The Battalion moved forward in the afternoon to E.26.a area, & again at night moved up to relieve the 1st Royal Irish Rifles in the line. Dispositions: Bn. H.Q. J.26.a.0595; "C" Coy. J.26.b.61; "A" Coy. J.26.b.88 area. "B" Coy. J.20.b.d central; "D" Coy. in reserve behind Battalion H.Q. | etc. |

# WAR DIARY
## or
## INTELLIGENCE SUMMARY.
(Erase heading not required.)

Army Form C. 2118.

VIII. 2nd. R. Inniskilling Fusiliers.

| Place | Date 1918 | Hour | Summary of Events and Information | Remarks and references to Appendices |
|---|---|---|---|---|
| | Oct. 24. | | Patrols had been ordered to advance at 01.00 in conjunction with 108 Brigade but since they did not move, our patrols could not go forward. The day was spent in these positions, the enemy shelling fairly heavily and sweeping all roads and approaches to the front line with Machine Gun fire. | etc |
| | Oct. 25. | | At about 02.00 the ½ 1st. Battalion took over the right sector of our line - J26 d 24 to J27a 24 - in preparation for an advance in the morning. The Battalion front was then held by "A" & "C" Coys. in the line, with "B" Coy. in support and "D" Coy. in reserve. At 09.00 they advanced behind a barrage with the 1st. Battalion on their right, and the 1st. Royal Irish Fusiliers on their left. The latter Battalion found great difficulty in going forward, and finally stopped, causing this Battalion to stop also on a line J27a 95.95 - J33 b 31 - J33 a 32. | etc |

# WAR DIARY or INTELLIGENCE SUMMARY

**Army Form C. 2118.**

IX. 2nd Royal Inniskilling Fusiliers.

| Place | Date 1918 | Hour | Summary of Events and Information | Remarks and references to Appendices |
|---|---|---|---|---|
| | | | At 14.00 the attack was resumed under a barrage, but finding enfilade fire from Machine Guns on the left the Battalion withdrew again to the line it had started from, causing the 1st Battalion on our right to do the same. Finally the line, after some re-adjustment with the 1st Battalion, stopped at J34a38 - J27d 9595 - J27b 05 where liaison was established with the 1st Royal Irish Fusiliers on the left. | etc. |
| | Oct. 26. | | The night of the 25/26th was fairly quiet & was occupied in bringing up stores etc. Occupied in bringing up stores etc. A letter of congratulation received from the Army Commander and also one from the Divisional Commander, on the good work which the Division had done. | etc. etc. |
| | Oct. 27. | | Orders received that the Battalion would be relieved by the 2/4 Battn. Queens on the night of the 27th/28th. Preparations were being made for the relief when, at about 15.30, a civilian was sent down to Battalion H.Q., having come in to our lines through "C" Coy. He declared that the enemy was evacuating, so | etc. |

**WAR DIARY**
or
INTELLIGENCE SUMMARY.
(Erase heading not required.)

Army Form C. 2118.

2nd. Royal Inniskilling Fusiliers

| Place | Date 1918. | Hour | Summary of Events and Information | Remarks and references to Appendices |
|---|---|---|---|---|
| | Oct. 28. | | Patrols were pushed forward and the Battalion again advanced in conjunction with the 1st. Battalion to J28 91 - J28a central - J34 & 89, on which line, owing to the darkness and an exposed left flank, they consolidated. Here they were relieved by the 2/4th Queens, and the Battalion marched back to billets at B17d 94. | Etc. |
| | Oct. 28. | | The Battalion remained in billets resting and attended the baths at OYGHEM. | Etc. |
| | Oct. 29. | | The Battalion marched to fresh billets, skirting COURTRAI to St ANNE — N.19a where they were accommodated in and around a Convent. | Etc. |
| | Oct. 30 & 31. | | Were spent by the Battalion in resting and re-organising. | Etc. |

E.G. Crawford. Lt Col.
Commandg 2nd Roy Inniskilling Fus

# WAR DIARY
## or
## INTELLIGENCE SUMMARY.

*Army Form C. 2118.*

2nd Royal Inniskilling Fusiliers

| Place | Date | Hour | Summary of Events and Information | Remarks and references to Appendices |
|---|---|---|---|---|
| | October 1918 | | Appendix No. I. <br><br> Casualties while in the line at DADIZEELE. <br> To October 3rd. <br><br> OFFICERS.          OTHER RANKS. <br> WOUNDED.                          Killed. 6. <br> CAPT. J. HARDY, M.C., THE CONN. RANG. attd.    Missing. 10. <br> MAJOR GALLAGHER, D.S.O. THE MUNSTER FUS. attd.    Wounded. 40. <br><br> October 13th – 16th. <br><br> KILLED. <br> 2/LIEUT. F.A. SADLIER.                   Killed 19 <br> WOUNDED. <br> CAPT. A.C. LENDRUM, M.C.               Wounded 123 <br> LIEUT. F.W. LILLBURNE. <br> 2/LIEUT. W. NELSON.                      Missing 2. <br> 2/LIEUT. S.V. HOOD. | |

## WAR DIARY
## INTELLIGENCE SUMMARY

Army Form C. 2118.

| Place | Date | Hour | Summary of Events and Information | Remarks and references to Appendices |
|---|---|---|---|---|
| | | | October 23-27th. | |
| | | | OTHER RANKS. | |
| | | | Killed. 7. | |
| | | | Wounded. 57. | |
| | | | OFFICERS. | |
| | | | WOUNDED. | |
| | | | Capt. S.M.H. MARK. | |
| | | | Lieut. J.S. McCORRY. | |
| | | | 2/Lieut. J.W. ALLEN. | |
| | | | 2/Lieut. A.H. MARTIN. | |

# WAR DIARY

**2nd Royal Inniskilling Fusiliers**

Army Form C. 2118.

| Place | Date | Hour | Summary of Events and Information | Remarks and references to Appendices |
|---|---|---|---|---|
| | October 1918. | | | |
| | Oct. 2nd to October 2nd. | | Appendix No. 2. | |

Officers commanding the Battalion & Companies during October 1918.

**COMMANDING OFFICER.**

MAJOR GALLAGHER, D.S.O. Munster Fusiliers, attached. — Wounded.

MAJOR E.W. CRAWFORD, D.S.O. 9th Battn. R. Inniskilling Fusiliers.

**ADJUTANT.**

CAPT. T. MAGUIRE, M.C.

**COMPANY COMMANDERS.**

"A" Coy. 2/LT. (A/CAPT) LODGE, M.C. to October 18th.
CAPT. V.E.S. MATTOCKS. October 26th
CAPT. S.M.H. MARK from October 18th to October 23rd.

Army Form C. 2118.

# WAR DIARY
## or
## INTELLIGENCE SUMMARY.

*(Erase heading not required.)*

2nd Royal Inniskilling Fusiliers.

| Place | Date | Hour | Summary of Events and Information | Remarks and references to Appendices |
|---|---|---|---|---|
| "B" Coy. | | | Lieut. (A/Capt.) E.R. Barrett to October 2nd. Capt. Knox, October 2nd. | |
| "C" Coy. | | | Capt. J. Hardy, M.C. to October 2nd. Wounded. Lieut. (A/Capt.) E.R. Barrett from October 2nd. | |
| "D" Coy. | | | 2/Lieut Gorman to 7th October 6/15-21st Oct. Leave. Capt. Lendrum, M.C. from Oct. 7th to October 15th. Wounded. 2/Lieut. (M/Capt) Lodge, M.C. from 21st October. | |
| | | | Signalling Officer. Lieut. Kerswill from Oct. 21. | |
| | | | Intelligence Officer. Lieut. Lillburne, The Connaught Rang. attd. from Oct. 1 to Oct. 14. Wounded. 2/Lieut. W.G. Eason, from Oct. 15. | |

# WAR DIARY or INTELLIGENCE SUMMARY

Army Form C. 2118.

2nd Royal Inniskilling Fusiliers

## Appendix No. 3.

Decorations awarded to Officers and Men of the Battalion during the month of October, 1918.

### BAR TO MILITARY CROSS.

2/Lieut (A/Capt.) T. Maguire, M.C.

### MILITARY CROSS.

2/Lieut. E. H. Lodge.
Lieut (A/Capt.) P. J. Dunworth.

### MILITARY MEDAL.

No. 7446 C.S.M. Hanna, J., "A" Coy.  No. 19702 Sgt. McIntyre, D., "B" Coy.
No. 29429 Pte. Hassard, A., "C" Coy.  43873 Pte. Cullinane, T., "A" Coy.
No. 30555 Pte. Hutchinson, A., "C" Coy.

### BAR TO MILITARY MEDAL.

No. 2466 Pte. McDowell, A., "C" Coy.

E. G. Crawford, Lt. Col.
Comm 2nd Roy Inniskilling Fus.

War Diary
of the
2nd. Bn. Royal Inniskilling Fusiliers,
for the month of
November, 1918.

E.C. Crawford
Lt. Col. Comdg.,
2nd Bn. R. Inniskilling Fus.

Army Form C. 2118.

Instructions regarding War Diaries and Intelligence Summaries are contained in F.S. Regs., Part II. and the Staff Manual respectively. Title pages will be prepared in manuscript.

# WAR DIARY
## or
## INTELLIGENCE SUMMARY

(Erase heading not required.)

Army Form C. 2118.

2nd Bn. Royal Inniskilling Fusiliers

| Place | Date | Hour | Summary of Events and Information | Remarks and references to Appendices |
|---|---|---|---|---|
| ST. ANNE. | November 1st. | | In billets in the CONVENT, ST. ANNE. Commanding Officers' Parade, Company Parades and Baths occupy most of the day. | |
| | 2nd. | | Training according to programme of work. | |
| | 3rd. | | Sunday. Church Parades as usual for services in 9th Battalion billets. Notification received that the MILITARY MEDAL has been awarded to the following N.C.O's and men :— 29246 Pte. J. Degnan. 21045 Pte. E. O'Neill. 49721 L/Cpl. H. Renwick. 15690 Sgt. L. Kirby. 14091 Sgt. R. McClintock. 24196 L/Cpl. J. Russell. 41583 Pte. F. Pearson. 22838 L/Cpl. J. Bell. | |
| | 4th. | | Training according to programme of work. | |
| | 5th. | | Adjutant's Parade and a Commanding Officers' Parade for Ceremonial Drill. This day a Side Drum which had been lost at BEAUVOIS during the retirement on the 26th August, 1914, was returned to the Battalion, having been found in a barn at BEAUVOIS by the 1st NEW ZEALAND BRIGADE during an advance. The instrument | |

# WAR DIARY or INTELLIGENCE SUMMARY

2nd Bn. Royal Inniskilling Fusiliers.

| Place | Date | Hour | Summary of Events and Information | Remarks and references to Appendices |
|---|---|---|---|---|
| | November | | was in perfect order, having been cased by a cover, and a letter of thanks was sent to the 1st NEW ZEALAND BRIGADE for returning it. In the evening a concert and cinema show was held in the 9th Battalions billets. | |
| | 6th. | | Rain put an early end to the usual "Programme of Work". | |
| | 7th. | | Practice Ceremonial Parade for inspection by Corps Commander. | |
| | 8th. | | More Rain. | |
| | 9th. | | Inspection of 109th INFANTRY BRIGADE by the Corps Commander, LIEUT. GENERAL R.B. STEPHENS. Presentation of medals to the following:- | |
| | | | BAR TO MILITARY CROSS.  CAPT. T. MAGUIRE, M.C. | |
| | | | BAR TO MILITARY MEDAL.  No. 2446 PTE. A. McDOWELL. | |
| | | | MILITARY MEDAL.  7746. C.S.M. J. HANNA.  14091 SGT. R. McCLINTOCK.  15646 SGT. G. JOHNSTON.  15640 SGT. L. KIRBY. | |

Army Form C. 2118.

# WAR DIARY
## or
## INTELLIGENCE SUMMARY.  2nd Bn. R. Inniskilling Fusiliers

(Erase heading not required.)

| Place | Date | Hour | Summary of Events and Information | Remarks and references to Appendices |
|---|---|---|---|---|
| | November | | | |
| | | | MILITARY MEDAL. No. 28399. CPL. W. McNERLIN  49421 L/CPL. H. RENNICK. | |
| | | | 24196. L/CPL. J. RUSSELL. 42026 L/CPL. A. AINSWORTH. | |
| | | | 22838. L/CPL. J. BELL. 21683. L/CPL. W. BRADLEY. | |
| | | | 29246. PTE. J. DEGNAN. 29729. PTE. A. HASSARD. | |
| | | | 45169. PTE. A. SMITH. 8149. PTE. J. RUSSELL. | |
| | | | 21045. PTE. E. O'NEILL. | |
| | | | The Corps Commander expressed great satisfaction with the general | Adj |
| | | | turn out and soldier-like appearance of the parade. | |
| | 10th | | Sunday. Church Parade in 9th Battalions Billets. About 20.00 the sky | |
| | | | was noticed to be lit up with searchlights and rockets and a rumour began | |
| | | | that the Armistice had been signed. Although it was not actually signed till | |
| | | | the following day the Band and many of the Battalion turned out and paraded | |
| | | | along the roads to Brigade Head Quarters to celebrate the occasion | Adj |
| | 11th | | Officers newsreceived then the Armistice had been signed by Germany. | Adj |
| | 12th | | No work was done to-day. | Adj |
| | | | Training under Company arrangements. | |

Army Form C. 2118.

# WAR DIARY
# INTELLIGENCE SUMMARY.   2nd Bn. Royal Inniskilling Fusiliers.
(Erase heading not required.)

| Place | Date | Hour | Summary of Events and Information | Remarks and references to Appendices |
|---|---|---|---|---|
| | November. | | | |
| | 13th. | | Training under Company arrangements. The following awards were published in Divisional Routine Orders — | |
| | | | SECOND BAR TO MILITARY CROSS,  REV. J.G. PATON, M.C., A.C.D., attd. | |
| | | | BAR TO MILITARY CROSS,  CAPT. A.C. LENDRUM, M.C. | |
| | | | MILITARY CROSS,  CAPT. W.H. KNOX, CONN. RANG., attd. | |
| | | | CAPT. E.R. BARRETT, R. DUBLIN FUS., attd. | |
| | | | 2/LT. W. NELSON. | |
| | | | DISTINGUISHED CONDUCT MEDAL.  42027. PTE. R. GREEN. | |
| | | | 49734. PTE. J. HUTCHINSON. | |
| | 14th. | | Battalion took part in a ten mile Brigade Route March. | |
| | 15th. | | The Battalion moved from ST. ANNE to billets in RONCQ, on the main MENIN-LILLE Rd. Billets were easily found for all owing to the number of unoccupied houses, and dismantled flax factories provided Recreation Rooms, School Rooms, Stores, etc. | |
| | 16th. | | The Commanding Officer lectured the Battalion in the Recreation Room, on | |

Army Form C. 2118.

# WAR DIARY
## or
## INTELLIGENCE SUMMARY
(Erase heading not required.)

2nd Bn. Royal Inniskilling Fusiliers

| Place | Date | Hour | Summary of Events and Information | Remarks and references to Appendices |
|---|---|---|---|---|
| | November | | some of the problems of Demobilisation. Divisional Routine Order No. 2480 — "His Majesty the King has approved of the award of the VICTORIA CROSS to No. 2364 L/Cpl. ERNEST SEAMAN, late 2nd R. Inniskilling Fus." | GOC |
| | 17th | | Thanksgiving service in Roubaix which was attended by representatives of the Army. Captain E. R. Barrett, M.C., 2/Lt. S. Olivier, & 2/Lt. R. S. Gorman representing this Battalion with a party of 75 other ranks. Unfortunately this detachment was unable to attend the service owing to the late arrival of the buses, but arrived in time to take part in the march past the Army Commander in the square of Roubaix. A congratulatory message was received from the Divisional Commander and the Brigade Commander on the appearance of the detachment. | GOC |
| | 18th | | Training according to programme of work. | |

Army Form C. 2118.

# WAR DIARY
or
~~INTELLIGENCE~~ SUMMARY.
*(Erase heading not required.)*

Instructions regarding War Diaries and Intelligence Summaries are contained in F.S. Regs., Part II. and the Staff Manual respectively. Title pages will be prepared in manuscript.

2nd Bn. Royal Inniskilling Fusiliers

| Place | Date | Hour | Summary of Events and Information | Remarks and references to Appendices |
|---|---|---|---|---|
| | November 19 - 26. | | Training according to the Programme of Work, varied by attacks by the Brigade on the village of LINSELLES. In the afternoons Cross Country Running & Inter-Company and Battalion football matches, vary the monotony. The school is now in full swing under 2/Lt. R.A. LOCKHART. Notification received of the following award – | |
| | 26th. | | THE MILITARY CROSS – CAPT. J. McCAW. | |
| | 27th - 30th. | | Still training according to a programme of work. | |

E.B. Crawford. Col.
Comm'g 2nd Bn The Roy Inniskilling Fusiliers

War Diary
of the
2nd Bn. Royal Inniskilling Fusiliers

for the month of December, 1918.

A. Hulse
Major, Comdg,
2nd Bn. R. Inniskilling Fus.

# WAR DIARY or INTELLIGENCE SUMMARY

Army Form C. 2118.

2nd Bn. R. Inniskilling Fus.

Vol 5

| Place | Date | Hour | Summary of Events and Information | Remarks and references to Appendices |
|---|---|---|---|---|
| December 1, 1918 | | | In billets in RONCQ. The usual training is being carried out with plenty of sport in the afternoons. | |
| | 2. | | | |
| | 3. | | The Battalion takes part in a Brigade attack on QUESNOY | |
| | 4 & 5 | | Usual training | |
| | 6. | | Performance of the cinema in the evening. Divisional Parade on the flying ground at HALLUIN, | |
| | | | and inspection had to be cancelled owing to Learyriver to the satisfaction of all. Interior Economy - a cross country Run of 3½ miles with a fringe of 2.5 Francs to the winning day & £ with the runs. | |
| | 7. | | | |
| | 8. | | "The following party left for England, to bring back the Regimental Colours - Capt. T. MAGUIRE, M.C. 2/Lt. A.C.G. ROGERS. No. 8323 C.Q.M.S. M. MAHAFFY; No. 8368 C.Q.M.S. J. HOPKINS; No. 6462 CORPL. H. MAGEE. Training awarding to a programme of work. Notification received of the following awards:- | |
| | 9. | | FRENCH CROIX DE GUERRE à l'ordre Corps (GOLDEN STAR) LT. COL. E.W. CRAWFORD D.S.O. à l'ordre Brigade (BRONZE STAR) — CAPT. JAMEGAW M.C. | |
| | | | Do. Do. | |

# WAR DIARY
## or
## INTELLIGENCE SUMMARY.
(Erase heading not required.)

2nd. Bn. R. Inniskilling Fus.

Army Form C. 2118.

| Place | Date | Hour | Summary of Events and Information | Remarks and references to Appendices |
|---|---|---|---|---|
| | | | FRENCH CROIX DE GUERRE awarded Regiment (BRONZE STAR) — | |
| | | | 15670 SERGT L. KIRBY. | |
| | | | 49434. L/Cpl. J. HUTCHINSON. | |
| | | | 42624 PTE R. GREEN. | |
| | 10. | | The Battn. took part in a Brigade exercise. | |
| | 11. | | A lecture by Col. G.S. BOURNE on "Settlement of Soldiers on the land." | |
| | | | The future of the Brigade cross country run in which to Battn. Team ran very well but did not come home first. | |
| | 12. | | A party of 8 MINERS, proceeding to be Discharged except for Demobilisation is in favourable ones. He made programme of work is carried out by those who are left. | |
| | 13. | | A lecture in MOUSCRON by Mr. H. DUBERY on "Industries" was attended by Representatives of the Bn. The subject proved for first time being advance & namely the company for Going out ammu- with wire Gauntlets to pull the stakes out of the barbed wire entanglements which encircle most of the villages in the district. | |

Army Form C. 2118.

# WAR DIARY
## or
## INTELLIGENCE SUMMARY.  2nd Bn. R. Inniskilling

(Erase heading not required.)

2nd Bn. R. Inniskilling Fus.

| Place | Date | Hour | Summary of Events and Information | Remarks and references to Appendices |
|---|---|---|---|---|
| December/18 | 14. | | Another party of Miners proceed to the Dispersal Camp. | |
| | 15. | | The usual Church Parades | |
| | 16. | | The Divisional Parade which was to have been held on the 6th took | |
| | | | place to day, the Divisions marching past Lt. Gen. Sir B. DeLisle, K.C.B. | |
| | 17-21. | | The Bn. carried out the usual training. The 35th E.O.M. Coy. fitted the | |
| | | | principal messes & huts with electric light which is a great improvement | |
| | | | of the shortage & price of candles. On the 18th the Colour Party returned with the Colours which were received with the | Ceremony in the Mess |
| | | | The Brigade Boxing contests took place followed by an | |
| | 21. | | exhibition by Sergt. Johnny Summers R.I. | |
| | | | Church Parades as usual. | |
| | 22. | | The Bn. carried out the usual training, & at the same time | |
| | 23 & 24. | | busy in decorating their dining halls for Xmas & making all the | |
| | | | necessary preparation. Each Coy. desired to have a dining hall of their own | |
| | | | & thanks principally to the Quartermaster, Lt. D.J. Bell, & the many friends of the | |
| | | | Battn. at home an excellent dinner is prepared. | |
| | 25. | | Xmas Day. Church services in the morning & at 1.30 the Battn. are | |

# WAR DIARY
## or
## INTELLIGENCE SUMMARY.
*(Erase heading not required.)*

Army Form C. 2118.

| Place | Date | Hour | Summary of Events and Information | Remarks and references to Appendices |
|---|---|---|---|---|
| | | | to the "Boys Xmas" dinner. Col. Hewitt of the M.G.C., sometime "D" Coy. Comdr. of this Bn., paid us a visit & went round the dinners with Lt. Col. CRAWFORD getting a great reception from the men, especially those of the transport, many of whom remembered him. On being asked to award the prize of 50 francs to the boy whose dining hall was best decorated, he awarded it to "A" Coy. | |
| | 26. | | No parades to-day except for a innate Roll Call. | |
| | 27. | | Xord. gathering. MAJOR A. HULSE of the 9th. Bn. assumed command of the Bn. in the absence of LT. Col. E.W. CRAWFORD D.S.O., on leave. | |
| | 28. | | Church Parade as usual. | |
| | 29 & 30. | | The usual training, Baths, Xord. gathering & ashore. | |
| | 31. | | A Cross Country Run for the Bn., which was attended by everyone. The Band played out the boys of 1918 & played in 1919. | |

A. Hulse Major, Comdg.
2nd Bn. R. Inniskilling Fus.

Army Form C. 2118.

# WAR DIARY
## or
## INTELLIGENCE SUMMARY.
(Erase heading not required.)

2nd Bn. Royal Inniskilling Fusiliers.

| Place | Date | Hour | Summary of Events and Information | Remarks and references to Appendices |
|---|---|---|---|---|
| | January 3rd 1919. 3 - 4th | | Battalion still in billets in RONCQ, but gradually drifting away & "demobilised". Training consists for the most part of squad drilling & route marches. | E. |
| | 5th. | | Usual Church Parades in the Cinema Hall. | E. |
| | 6th. | | Battalion Route March through HALLUIN and LINSELLES. | E. |
| | 7th. | | Educational & Recreational Training & Ceremonial Drill. | E. |
| | 8th. | | Football match against the 36th Div. M.T. Coy. which resulted in a win for us by 11 goals to 1. Cinema at night | E. |
| | 9th. | | Lecture by the A.D.M.S in the Cinema, and also by Professor SECOMBE on the LEAGUE of NATIONS and DEMOCRACY. | E. |
| | 10th & 11th. | | The usual routine, with a football match against the 108th Infy. Brigade on the afternoon of the 11th. This Brigade was represented by the 16th R.I. Rifles and the match resulted in a win for us by 2 goals to nil. | E. |
| | 12th | | Church Parades as usual. A party of 50 O.R's & 2Lt. G.H.CLARKE attended a Service in ROUBAIX. | E. |

# WAR DIARY
## INTELLIGENCE SUMMARY

2nd Bn. R. Inniskilling Fusiliers

Army Form C. 2118.

| Place | Date | Hour | Summary of Events and Information | Remarks and references to Appendices |
|---|---|---|---|---|
| | | | The BELGIAN CROIX DE GUERRE awarded to the following | |
| | | | MAJOR A. HULBE (9th Bn., temporarily in command of this Bn. during the absence of Lt. Col. E.W. CRAWFORD, D.S.O., on leave) | |
| | | | 7685. R.S.M. J. SNODDEN, D.C.M. 8366. C.S.M. S. GODFREY. | |
| | | | 3956. Pte. R. KANE. M.M. 15678. Pte. W. LAVERY. | |
| | | | 40630. L/Cpl. J. CARDLAN. | |
| | 13th. | | Usual routine. Lt. Col. E.W. Crawford D.S.O. returned from leave and took over command of Battalion | E. |
| | 14th. | | A BRIGADE Ceremonial Parade on the Parade Ground of the 1st Bn. to practise for the presentation of colours to the 9th Bn., and the march past. | E. |
| | 15th. | | Usual routine, with a concert by the "DANDIES" in the Cinema Hall in the evening. | E. |
| | 16th. | | Ditto, with a performance by the 108th FIELD AMBULANCE in the evening. | E. |
| | 17th, 19th & 20th. | | Usual routine. | E. |
| | 18th. | | Do. Brigade Tug of War Competition on 1st Bn. ground in which we were beaten by the 9th Bn. | E. |
| | 21st. | | A BRIGADE Ceremonial Parade on the which the colours were carried, and | E. |

Army Form C. 2118.

# WAR DIARY
## or
## INTELLIGENCE SUMMARY.
(Erase heading not required.)

2nd Bn. R. Inniskilling Fusiliers

| Place | Date | Hour | Summary of Events and Information | Remarks and references to Appendices |
|---|---|---|---|---|
| | 22nd | | A short address was given to the parade by Brig. General HESSEY on the subject of the Colours and their history. Usual routine with a Concert by the "SIEGE SINGERS" in the evening which was not exactly appreciated. Notification of the award of the MERITORIOUS SERVICE MEDAL to — 6039 R.Q.M. Sergt. A.L.V. McLAREN. 4446. C.S.M. W. HANNA, M.M. 8086. C.S.M. J. FLEMING. | 6. 6. |
| | 23rd 26th | | Usual routine. | 6. |
| | 27th | | LT. GENERAL SIR B. DE LISLE, K.C.B., D.S.O., presented a silk Union Flag to the 9th Battn. in the Drill Hall of the 2nd Bn. The ceremony which was to have been held out in the open had to be held indoors owing to a heavy fall of snow. After the presentation Service and the presentation the Brigade marched past GENERAL DE LISLE on their way back to billets. | |
| | 28th 31st | | Usual routine. If wood picking etc. On the 29th Miss LENA ASHWELLS Concert party gave a most enjoyable performance in the Cinema Hall. | 6. |
| | 31st | | H.R.H. The Prince of Wales honoured the Brigade with a visit in the | 6. |

# WAR DIARY
## or
## INTELLIGENCE SUMMARY

**Army Form C. 2118.**

2nd Bn. R. Inniskilling Fusiliers

Afternoon. I visited the Companies or play.

E.W. Crawford
Lt.Col.
Comdg 2nd/13th The Royal Inniskilling Fusiliers

APPENDIX.

Officers demobilised during the month of January, 1919.

2/Lt. T. FARNELL   S. STAFFS. attd.
M/Capt. J. McCAW, M.C.
Capt. J. COLHOUN, M.C.
2/Lt. J.H. CLARKE
2/Lt. E.S. GILLILAND

# WAR DIARY
## INTELLIGENCE SUMMARY

Army Form C. 2118.

2nd Bn. the Royal Inniskilling Fusiliers.

Vol 55

| Place | Date 1919 | Hour | Summary of Events and Information | Remarks and references to Appendices |
|---|---|---|---|---|
| RONCQ | 1st Feb | | Battalion still in billets at RONCQ. 3 other ranks proceeded to Camp for Demobilization. | |
| | 2nd | | Usual Church parade in the cinema hall. | |
| | 3rd | | Capt N.H. Knox M.C. and Lieut R.A. Lockhart with 5 other ranks proceeded to Concentration Camp for Demobilization. | |
| | 4th | | Series Country run in the morning, football match in the afternoon. 'C' Coy v 11th: 1 Coy 9th Bn. final of inter-Coy Competition. Result after playing extra time 'C' Coy 1 goal 9th Coy 1 goal. The match, played in a blinding snowstorm from a most exciting one. | |
| | 5th | | The usual Runs among the morning. The drawn football match C Coy v N.I. Coy 9th was played during the afternoon, resulting in a win for C Coy 2nd Bn by 3 goals to 0. Brigadier Genl L.J. Wray C.B. presented a very nice silver Cup on conclusion of the match. Complimenting the teams on their splendid play. 8 other ranks proceeded to Concentration Camp for Demobilization. | |

Army Form C. 2118.

# WAR DIARY
or
# INTELLIGENCE SUMMARY.
(Erase heading not required.)

2nd Bn The Royal Inniskilling Fusiliers

Instructions regarding War Diaries and Intelligence Summaries are contained in F. S. Regs., Part II. and the Staff Manual respectively. Title pages will be prepared in manuscript.

| Place | Date 1919 | Hour | Summary of Events and Information | Remarks and references to Appendices |
|---|---|---|---|---|
| RONCQ | 5th Jany | | A draft of 80 other Ranks proceeded to join the 7/8 R. Inniskilling Fus. at BOULOGNE. This draft was composed of those who had joined the colours on or subsequent to 1st Jany 1916. | |
| | 6th | | Training & Hand Collecting was carried out. 8 other Ranks | E |
| | | | proceed to Concentration Camp for Demobilization | E |
| | 7th | | Training was carried out under Coy. arrangements. by 2 Coys, while 2 Coys were engaged Collecting wood for fuel purposes. Lieut JA Awley M.O. and 21 W.O. N.C.Os. proceed to Concentration Camp for Demobilization. The Band under Bandmaster L.S. Grigg Consisting of 23 other ranks joined Bn from England. | E |
| | 8th | | The usual Recreational, Educational & Drill training carried out. 4 O.R. proceeded to Concentration Camp for Demobilization | E |
| | 9th | | Band Church (parade) Service. The Band of the Bn employed in collecting wood for fuel purposes. | E |
| | 10th | | All available men were engaged in Collecting wood for fuel purposes. 12 O.R. proceed to Concentration Camp for Demob. | E |
| | 11th | | Coys were engaged in the usual Recreational & Educational training. 18 O.R. demobilized | E |

# WAR DIARY
## or
## INTELLIGENCE SUMMARY.
*(Erase heading not required.)*

2nd Royal Inniskilling Fusiliers

Army Form C. 2118.

| Place | Date 1919 | Hour | Summary of Events and Information | Remarks and references to Appendices |
|---|---|---|---|---|
| RONCQ | 12th & 13th | | Educational recreational training and drill carried out. 3 O.R. Demobilized | |
| | 13th | | All available men engaged in woodcollecting for fuel purposes. | |
| | | | 38 O.R. rank proceeded to Inoculation Camp to Demobilize. | Q |
| | 14th | | Boys were placed at disposal of A.S.C. brigade. 20 O.R. Demobilized | Q |
| | 15th | | Hon'al Divine Service | Q |
| | 16th | | Owing to fitting Engines on Lorries or Limbers and ammunition dumps here rendered very few men available for training. Rest were employed in variety of transport work clearing vehicles re. the transport personnel lorries fallen away transferred to Dunkerque. | Q |
| | 17th & 18th | | Signed collecting & Bathing. | Q |
| | 19th | | The usual routine of training carried out. 9 O.R. Demobilized | Q |
| | 20th | | Bathing & Recreational training. | Q |
| | 21st | | Coys under the O.C. Commanding for Interior Economy. 11 O.R. Demobilized | Q |
| | 22nd | | Usual Routine of Recreational training. | Q |
| | 23rd | | Church Service. 22 O.R. Demobilized. {Employed R.G.A. in 5th Army football competition. Winning by 3 goals to 1. | Q |
| | 24th | | Usual routine. Working group party. Use of the phrase "In the field" discontinued. | |

# WAR DIARY
## or
## INTELLIGENCE SUMMARY.

2nd R. Inniskilling Fus.

Army Form C. 2118.

| Place | Date 1919 | Hour | Summary of Events and Information | Remarks and references to Appendices |
|---|---|---|---|---|
| RONCQ | 25th | | Usual parades. One O.R. demobilised. | E.G. |
| | 26th | | Ordinary daily routine. Football match in the afternoon Bn team (badly depleted in talent owing to Demobilisation) v 15th Bn MG Corps in VTH army compn. Bn. team beaten by 1 goal to 0 after playing extra time. | E.G. |
| | 27th | | Bn engaged in packing up - prior to move to MOUSCRON. | E.G |
| | 28th | | As for 27th. | E.G |
| | | | Total demobilised during month :- Officers 4 OR 146. Many of whom came to France with the Bn. in August 1914 and served continuously with it throughout the Campaign. | |

2.3.1919.

E.G.Crawford
Lt.Col.
Comm'g 2/B The Royal Inniskilling Fusiliers

Army Form C. 2118.

# WAR DIARY
## or
## INTELLIGENCE SUMMARY. 2nd Bn The R. Inniskilling Fus.
*(Erase heading not required.)*

| Place | Date 1919 | Hour | Summary of Events and Information | Remarks and references to Appendices |
|---|---|---|---|---|
| RONCQ | March 1st | | Moved to MOUSCRON, and on arrival found some difficulty in securing billets, as the move of the 12th R. Irish Rifles, whom the Bn. was to take over from, was postponed 24 hours. | |
| MOUSCRON | 2nd | | The usual Church parade. The Band of the Bn. supplying the music | |
| | 3rd | | Bn. employed in cleaning up and improving billets. A draft of 32 other ranks proceeded to join 7/8th at BOULOGNE, 3 other ranks proceeded to Concentration Camp to Demob. | |
| | 4th | | Usual routine - all ranks except 120 other ranks Bn men to take, withdrawn. | |
| | 5th | | " " Bn. football team travel out to play 10th K.O.S.B.'s | |
| | | | The 2nd round IV Corps Competition. K.O.S.B.'s Scratched. | |
| | 6-8 | | Usual routine. Bn. gave Concert in Cinema Hall Mouscron which was largely attended and wasn't appreciated | |
| | 9 | | Church parade. 29 other ranks proceeded to Concentration Camp for demobilisation | |
| | 10 | | Usual routine. | |
| | 11 | | " — Band outing to YPRES. and battlefield. | |

# WAR DIARY 2nd Bn. The R. Innis. Killing Fus.
## or
## INTELLIGENCE SUMMARY.

Army Form C. 2118.

(Erase heading not required.)

| Place | Date | Hour | Summary of Events and Information | Remarks and references to Appendices |
|---|---|---|---|---|
| MOUSCRON | March 9th 1919 | | | |
| | 12 | | C. in C. (Sir Douglas Haig K.T. &c.) visited 36th Divn. Hd. Qrs. and interviewed staff and Officers Commanding Units | |
| | 13-14 | | Usual daily routine | 6 |
| | 15 | | Bn. Football Team proceeded by lorry to OUDENARDE to play a match in 3rd round XI Corps Competition | 6 |
| | 16 | | Usual Church Parade. All ranks looking out for English Mail, as up to date no Shamrock for St. Patrick's day had arrived. Bn. football team beaten by 2nd Bde R.G.A. in 3rd round of Corps Competition. Score 1-0. | 6 |
| | 17th | | St. Patrick Day Bde Sports arranged were cancelled, owing to the departure of the C.O. of the 1st Bn. to U.K. after having served exactly 3 years in France + Belgium. Dance organized by the Bn. proved a great success. Music supplied by the Band of the Bn. | 6 |
| | 18th | | Usual routine | 6 |
| | 19th | | Brig. Gen. N.F. Albany Bde Comdg. 107th Bde proceeded home. The Band of the Bn. played him away from Bde Hd. Qrs. His departure was regretted | 6 |

# WAR DIARY 4th. The Royal Inniskilling Fus.
## or
## INTELLIGENCE SUMMARY.
*(Erase heading not required.)*

Army Form C. 2118.

| Place | Date 1919 March | Hour | Summary of Events and Information | Remarks and references to Appendices |
|---|---|---|---|---|
| MOUSCRON | 19 | | by all ranks of the Bn. in which he was universally popular. | |
| | 20-21 | | All other ranks proceeded to join 7/8 Bn. at BOULOGNE. Usual routine. The Divnl Commander (Major Genl. L. Coffin V.C. C.B. D.S.O.) paid a farewell visit to the Bn. Thanking them for the assistance given him while commanding the 36th Division. It will be remembered that the 21st March is the 1st anniversary of the big Boche push, which ultimately ended in disaster to himself. | E |
| | 22 | | Usual routine. 1 Officer and 12 other ranks proceeded to Genestration Camp for Army Course. | E |
| | 23 | | Usual routine. Church parade. Corps Commander (Lt. Genl. Sir Beauvoir De Lisle K.C.B.) visited Divnl. H.Q. also interviewed and bade goodbye to Unit Commander. | E |
| | 24 | | Usual routine. Bn. Equipment inspected by D.A.D.O.S. 7 O.R. proceeded to join 7/8 Bn. at BOULOGNE. | E |
| | 25-26 | | Usual routine. Many rumours current as to date of departure of Cadre of Bn. | E |

**WAR DIARY** 2nd Bn. The R. Inniskilling Fus. Army Form C. 2118.

or

**INTELLIGENCE SUMMARY.**

(Erase heading not required.)

| Place | Date | Hour | Summary of Events and Information | Remarks and references to Appendices |
|---|---|---|---|---|
| MOUSCRON | 28 | | Honours + Awards :- | |
| | | | Y/Lieut. Qm D.J BELL awarded CHEVALIER de L'ORDRE de la COURONNE and CROIX-de-GUERRE. No 816 Sgt J. O'NEILL awarded CHEVALIER de L'ORDRE du LEOPOLD II and CROIX-de-GUERRE | |
| " | 29-30 | | Usual Routine | |
| " | 31 | | " - Lieut. R S CORMAN and no other Rank proceeded to Gravenhage Camp for Demobilization - | |

MOUSCRON }
31. 3. 19 } Comdg. 2nd Bn. The R. Inniskilling Fus.

C W Crawford
Lt Colonel
Comdg. 2nd Bn. The R. Inniskilling Fus.

Demobilized during month Capt. E. R. Bennett, Lieut. R.S. Gorman + 45 OR
Transferred to 7/8 Bn R. Inniskilling Fus. during month 50. OR.

# WAR DIARY 2/m 2th R Inniskilling F. Army Form C. 2118.
## or INTELLIGENCE SUMMARY.
*(Erase heading not required.)*

| Place | Date 1919 April | Hour | Summary of Events and Information | Remarks and references to Appendices |
|---|---|---|---|---|
| MOUSCRON | 1 | | Usual daily routine | |
| " | 2 | | Officers 36th (Ulst.) Division gave a ball in the Hotel - de-ville Mouscron which was attended by a large number of Officers with their civilian friends. Dancing was kept up till the still small hours of the morning. | Ceased |
| " | 3-4 | | Usual Routine. 2nd Lieut. D.W. O'TOOLE R. Munsters Fus attached proceeded to concentration camp for Demobilisation. | |
| " | 5-11 | | Ordinary routine work by (Cadre of) the 93 other Ranks received to concentration camps for Demobilisation. The following awards for service in the field approved by Public Authorities:- Decoration Militaire without bars- Reserve to No 10599 Sgt P. RONAN and No 4029 PO H.S.WHEATLEY | |
| " | 12 | | Usual Routine - Football Match between Cadre of Bn and that of 15th R. Irish Rifles resulted in a win for us 6-7 to R.I.R. 0 | |
| " | 13 | | Usual Divine Service - In the afternoon football match played R. Irish Rifles. Winning by 13 Goals to 0. | |

# WAR DIARY 2nd Bn. R. Inniskilling Army Form C. 2118.
## or
## INTELLIGENCE SUMMARY.
*(Erase heading not required.)*

| Place | Date 1919 April | Hour | Summary of Events and Information | Remarks and references to Appendices |
|---|---|---|---|---|
| MOUSCRON | 14-16 | | Nothing of interest to chronicle | |
| " | 17 | | Cadre played football match against Divn. F. Amb. winning by 1 goal to 0. | |
| " | 18-19 | | Usual Routine | |
| " | 20 | | Easter Sunday. | |
| " | 21 | | Observed as a holiday | |
| " | 22-25 | | Usual Routine. 30th. Ranks proceeded to join 7/8 Bn. at BOULOGH= | |
| " | 26 | | Divnl. Sports, which owing to heavy rain had to be abandoned after the 3rd event. Of the 3 events run off the Cadre of the Bn took places as follows. 1st and 2nd in the 100 yards. 3rd in the ¼ mile race and 1st in the Dogs-of-war. | |
| " | 27-30 | | Usual Routine. Capt. T.P.W.Johnstone proceeded to join 3.31 P.O.W Coy. 9 Cpl. & 71 2nd guard Coy & Lieut. T King the O.C. & 9 Cpl. & W.B. 9 & 2nd guard Coy brought Reinfros attached and 2nd Lieut. W.M. Burns to XVII Corps proceeded to join 315 P.O.W. Coy. The Bn was reduced to Cadre on 15th April 1919. | |

MOUSCRON
30-4-19

Otto Graford Lt. Colonel
Commanding 2nd Bn. The R. Inniskilling Fus.

www.ingramcontent.com/pod-product-compliance
Lightning Source LLC
Chambersburg PA
CBHW081552160426
43191CB00011B/1912